RESTORED

You Can Recover All

Paulette Reed

RESTORED – YOU CAN RECOVER ALL

Copyright © 2018   Paulette Reed

Published by Paulette Reed Ministries

paulettereed.com

ISBN: 978-1-62166-802-2

RESTORED

Dedication

To all of those around the world who have been robbed by the enemy, may this book guide you to God's promises and bring you restoration and abundant life. May it fill you with hope as you walk with our Restorer – His name is Jesus.

To my three precious sons, daughters-in-law and perfect grandchildren, who always believe in me even when my journey seems like Abraham's, who trusted God and made bold moves, though he knew not where he was going. Your love keeps my dreams and hopes alive. Love never fails.

To my beautiful Lord and Savior who set my feet upon a rock, restored me to wholeness and filled me with joy unspeakable. "My heart overflows with a good theme; I address my verses to the King; My tongue is the pen of a ready writer" (Psalm 45:1).

Table of Contents

Introduction

Do you ever look back over the years and think, "Wow, I sure lost some things that were precious to me. I wish I could have them back..."? Well, I have good news; you *can* have them back! John 10:10 tells us that the enemy (the devil) comes to *steal*, but Jesus came to give you abundant life. All of God's promises are yes and amen, and they *will* come to pass. God is not a man that he should lie (Numbers 23:19), and His promises in the Bible include restoration – you are no exception.

I have experienced the wonderful benefits of restoration in the midst of brokenness and despair, and I shout from the rooftops today, "God restores!" I stand amazed as I look at my life and watch *perpetual restoration* all around me. As I look at my home, I see beautiful furniture and I remember that, at one point in time, I used cardboard boxes for end tables. I see a nice car in the garage – such a wonderful, restorative gift from God – which replaced a car that had major problems and was unsafe to drive. I rejoice because the Lord restored my health after picking up a virus in a foreign country. Education and the love of learning were restored as I attended college in midlife and the Master Teacher filled me with a hunger for knowledge so that I would grow and flourish; if we're not growing, we're stagnating.

Restoration of family relationships, friendships, love, finances, joy – it's all available, waiting for you to believe and receive from heaven.

Before you continue reading, pause for a few moments and ask God to fill *you* with hope and expectation, because happy is the man whose *hope is in the Lord* (Psalm 146:5). And expectation is your greenhouse for miracles. I'm talking about a spiritual greenhouse, where you can plant tiny seeds of hope and promise by faith. Matthew 17:20 says, "If you have faith the size of a mustard seed, you will say to this mountain, 'Move from here to there,' and it will move; and nothing will be impossible to you."

What mountain – obstacle – in your life do you need removed today? Come on; you certainly have faith the size of a teeny mustard seed, the smallest seed of all! When these seeds are watered with the Word of God and soaked in prayer, you will be amazed at how the Master Gardener makes them grow. If you truly believed that nothing is impossible for you and Jesus, how would you live differently? Ponder that in your heart for a while and expect the impossible things of God by faith. Ask the Lord to remove doubt and cynicism that has tried to attach itself to you following painful, emotional wounds, and replace every negative outcome from those wounds with love. That's what happened when Jesus was crucified for you and me ... the wounds on His hands and feet became wounds of love.

Are you ready for restoration, for blessings from the Almighty God of the universe? Think of it this way. If someone wanted to give you a million dollars, but you shunned the idea of the financial blessing because you didn't believe or expect it, do you think they would still give you a million dollars? Perhaps not. They would probably be compelled to gift the money to someone who had been praying and *expecting* the million dollars – someone standing ready to receive blessings [restoration] from God, steward the million dollars well and give God the glory. Make sure you are ready on the receiving end. Open your heart and position yourself to receive more than you can ask or imagine.

TIMES TWO

Wouldn't it be wonderful to have the good things the enemy stole restored, times two? Well, the Bible tells us that even that is possible. Take a look at one of God's many promises, found in Zechariah 9:12, "Return to the stronghold, you prisoners of hope. Even today I declare that I will restore double to you" (NKJV). Wow! Are you ready to receive double for your trouble?

I've traveled to developing nations, where so many people have lost so much that it's almost inconceivable. Thousands of people have experienced such horrendous trials and tribulations that they have even been robbed of hope. The dead, lifeless stare in their eyes is enough to bring anyone to tears ... and to their knees. While ministering in these nations, I looked around, and all I saw was poverty – totally destitute, aimless and lost men and women. It was as if there were no vision for the future, leaving these precious people empty. Why? Because without vision, people perish (Proverbs 29:18).

Stir up your faith today and get ready to recover all. May your hope be restored as you are restored. May your visions and dreams come alive, and your compassion and passion for life and the purposes of God be ignited or re-ignited as you read this book. Right now, right where you are, choose to believe that God truly is the Redeemer; that's what He does for a living, my friend, He redeems.

As you read, you may want to take time to pray and journal – let your thoughts and reflections flow. Journaling reveals what's in your heart, and God *reveals to heal*. I encourage you to also count your blessings and record your miraculous restorations, thanking God for them. Thankfulness increases faith because it reminds you that God's love never fails. He loves you and, oh, how He wants to bless you, so you will become a conduit of blessing to others. Listen, God longs to bless you. He created mankind and blessed it – and that includes you! You can recover all.

CHAPTER ONE

The River of Restoration

HELP ME, JESUS

Then he showed me a river of the water of life, clear as crystal, coming from the throne of God and of the Lamb, in the middle of its street. On each side of the river grew a tree of life, bearing twelve crops of fruit, with a fresh crop each month. The leaves were used for medicine to heal nations.

– Revelation 22:1-2

About twenty-five years ago I was in the midst of a painful divorce, my emotions were shattered, and my finances were wiped out. I felt betrayed and abandoned, was spiritually dead, paralyzed with anxiety, and was trying to raise my three precious sons to the best of my ability. I was broken, destitute, and empty. Talk about needing restoration!

Perhaps you can relate to needing restoration in some areas of your life. If so, I have great news for you. God has a river that flows from His throne, and He is inviting you to jump in. We can call this spiritual river a *river of restoration* because its waters are life-giving, it carries healing and restorative properties, and brings life to everything it touches. As we walk with the Lord on our journey of faith, we learn to flow with the leading of Holy Spirit and flow in this river that produces perpetual restoration, not only bringing healing and restoration to individuals but also to nations.

I have personally experienced the benefits of this river. During my brokenness and despair, God sent His River to restore me. And now, He's sending it to you.

AREAS THE RIVER RESTORES

JOY

In the midst of a season of depression and hopelessness, God led me into a "river encounter" where I was brought to sincere faith and filled with His Spirit. My entire being was flooded with the glory of God, and I heard Holy Spirit whisper to my heart, "Joy unspeakable." Now, this was before I even knew the promise in 1 Peter 1:8 which says,

> Though you have not seen Him, you love Him, and though you do not see Him now, but believe in Him, you greatly rejoice with joy inexpressible and full of glory.

Joy certainly didn't make sense to my mind due to my unhappy circumstances. Nevertheless, it was very real. At that moment God's joy became my strength. I have never lost this joy since; because the world didn't give it to me, the world can't take it away.

I love the Lord with all my heart, soul, and mind, and each morning His mercies are new. If you need more supernatural, unspeakable joy, ask God for it, and you will receive. And, don't forget that "the joy of the Lord is our strength" (Nehemiah 8:10). If you lose your eternal joy, you lose your strength.

PROVISION

I had lost everything through a painful divorce. The house, car, property and furniture were gone and there was little money to pay the bills. Isn't it wonderful to know that when we have nothing left but God, God is all we need? It was, and is, amazing to watch God restore provision.

Most often, it's during tough times – when it seems we have practically nothing – that God becomes our everything. Temporary lack is not a problem for God and He can use it to draw our hearts to Him so He can fill us with Himself, His glory and provision.

I remember moving into an old house that had some serious issues. The boys and I would set out at least ten buckets every time it rained because the roof was full of holes. The back door was broken and wouldn't lock, so the enemy used that to make me feel unsafe and torment me at nighttime. I could hear mice running inside the walls, which I hated so much!

However, when I went to church and joined in with fellow Spirit-filled believers – worshiping, praying, dancing and singing – I would totally forget all my problems. Sometimes when the pastor asked if anyone needed prayer I wouldn't raise my hand because at that moment in time, immersed in God's glory, it seemed I had no earthly problems.

It was during that season that I learned that God provides all our needs according to His riches in glory (Philippians 4:19). He longs to be our all-in-all and created us to be 100% dependent on Him. Wow, it only took me forty years to learn that lesson but, when I did I came out of the wilderness leaning on my Beloved. I learned to carry a song in my heart and both abide in His presence and be a carrier of His presence – His glory.

Oh, how I marvel at the Lord's goodness. His river is full of provision and it continues to increase.

PEACE

"I have peace like a river!" The Lord delivered me from anxiety through His wonderful River of Life and granted me divine peace that surpasses all human understanding. Of course, I still face challenges like everyone else, but I have supernatural peace that keeps me steady and strong through every trial.

If you're suffering from lack of peace, you are not alone. Well over 40 million children and adults in the United States alone suffer with you. Anxiety is one of the most prominent mental health issues in North America, and it's estimated that over one-third of the North American adult population experience anxiety-related health issues. Two of the top ten medications prescribed for panic attacks generate over five billion dollars a year in the United States alone. Wow!

How do we receive the supernatural peace of God?

For starters, always remember: The devil is a liar and God is Truth. Listen to God, and not the liar, and you will find peace. Philippians 4:7 promises you that, "The peace of God, which surpasses all comprehension, will guard your hearts and your minds in Christ Jesus."

Above all, we pray for it and our Heavenly Father deposits it in us. I am living proof of the Lord's restoration power – from being paralyzed by panic attacks to now preaching in front of thousands. I think it's impossible to explain the peace of God exactly, but I don't have to; I live it. I do believe it helps us to know that every crisis has a beginning and an end, and as we grow emotionally and spiritually, we can learn to ride the waves of life and not let them overtake us. Every wave that comes in, goes out.

Horatio G. Spafford knew peace that passes all human understanding. He was a successful lawyer and businessman in Chicago with a lovely family – a wife, Anna, and five children. However, they were not strangers to tears and tragedy. Their young son died with pneumonia in 1871, and in that same year, much of their business was lost in the Great Chicago Fire. Yet, God in His mercy and kindness allowed the business to flourish once more.

On Nov. 21, 1873, the French ocean liner, *Ville du Havre*, was crossing the Atlantic from the United States to Europe with 313 passengers on board. Among the passengers were Mrs. Spafford and their four daughters. Although Mr. Spafford had planned to travel with his family, at the last moment he had to stay in Chicago to help solve an unexpected business problem. He told his wife he would take another ship a few days later and join her and their children in Europe.

About four days into the crossing of the Atlantic, the *Ville du Havre* collided with a powerful, iron-hulled Scottish ship, the *Loch Earn*. Suddenly, all those on board were in grave danger. Anna hurriedly brought her four children to the deck. She knelt there with Annie, Maggie, Bessie and Tanetta and prayed that God would spare them and make them willing to endure whatever awaited them. Within approximately 12 minutes, the Ville du Havre slipped beneath the dark waters of the Atlantic, carrying with it 226 passengers, including the four Spafford children.

A sailor, rowing a small boat over the spot where the ship went down, spotted a woman floating on a piece of the wreckage. It was Anna, still alive. He pulled her into the boat and they were picked up by another large vessel which, nine days later, landed them in Cardiff, Wales. From there she wired her husband a message which began, "Saved alone, what shall I do?" Mr. Spafford later framed the telegram and placed it in his office.

Mr. Spafford booked passage on the next available ship and left to join his grieving wife. With the ship about four days out, the captain called Spafford to his cabin and told him they were over the place where his children went down.

According to Bertha Spafford Vester, a daughter born after the tragedy, Spafford wrote, "It Is Well with My Soul" while on this journey.

When peace like a river, attendeth my way,
When sorrows like sea billows roll,
Whatever my lot, Thou hast taught me to say,
It is well, it is well with my soul.

How amazing! Only God can give us supernatural peace like He did for Mr. Spafford. God restores our soul. He makes us lie down in green pastures, where there is delight and provision (Psalm 23).

HEALTH

The River brought healing to my physical body, mind, and emotions. Through sessions of prayer and inner healing, I was set free of anything and everything that was not from Jesus – I was restored to wholeness.

When God brings us healing, it is our responsibility to maintain it. If we don't love and take care of ourselves it's quite easy to put things into our bodies, minds and souls that can destroy us and sometimes others. Remember the second great commandment:

"Love your neighbor *as (you love) yourself.*" God's will is for you to love yourself, which implies taking care of yourself – and this will enable you to love and care for others. The opposite is also true. Why do you think some people hate their neighbors, or their nations for that matter? Because they hate themselves.

Be careful not to quickly jump to the conclusion that toxicity in the mind, soul or body is only the "other guy's" problem – the one who uses street drugs. There are millions of Christians who don't love and nurture themselves the way God intends, and they suffer the repercussions. We see a high rate of burnout in churches, ministries and corporations when lives are out of balance. People cannot serve others if they become an empty shell. "Work, play, rest" – write that down.

Years ago, a friend shared with me that he had set himself up for toxicity in his mind, causing him to have nightmares. I asked him what he meant by that and he went on to explain that he loved aviation. When he was young, he frequently watched dramatic movies where people were killed in violent airplane crashes. Now, as an adult, he consistently struggled with nightmares about ... you guessed it, violent airplane crashes. The good news is that once he recognized where he had opened the door to the violence flooding his soul, he was able to seek prayer and get free from the tormenting dreams. God reveals to heal.

One of my personal struggles is food – especially chocolate. I enjoy eating but, like anything else, when we overindulge, even a good thing becomes bad. Being overweight can cause severe health problems and even death, but we just don't talk about it freely like we do in the case of other "drugs."

God intended food to provide fuel for the body, not to stuff emotions. I remember one time following a crisis in my life I was overeating, and Holy Spirit whispered, "Paulette, I know your heart is hurting, but you're hurting your heart." Wow, God had my attention, and I said silently, "Thank You for never giving up on me, Lord. I am so sorry." We all have free will and again it's difficult, even for God, to restore our health if we're participating in self-sabotage. Sin promises pleasure but results in pain. I continue to press on, fighting the good fight. How about you? Hey, if you don't quit, you win.

COMMUNICATION

Last but not least, I had lost my ability to communicate and articulate well; it had been shut down. But when I encountered the River, my communication was restored. Since then, I have served the Body of Christ for many years as a prophetess, teacher, writer, and itinerant speaker. Yes, the River restores.

You, too, are called to communicate. You carry treasures and nuggets of truth that no one else carries. Each life-test that you pass creates a testimony to be celebrated and shared. When we overcome, it becomes our honor and responsibility to share with others how mighty our God is and how He helped us through our darkest hours. We can then teach how to overcome the very obstacles that tried to take us out. Whether it's to a nation or a neighbor – communicate. Don't let the devil silence your voice. Don't bow to panic and anxiety. Rise up and say, "I am going from a mess to a miracle. I am an overcomer!"

Sharing your story in writing, speaking, mailing cards, social media (or whatever method you choose) allows you to carry the torch for Jesus Christ. Determine to run with that torch and shout from the rooftops what God has done for you.

YOU'RE FURTHER DOWN THE ROAD
THAN YOU REALIZE

Many people don't realize how far they have come in life. Or perhaps they've backslidden and feel that has voided all their previous progress. But we serve the God of second chances, and third and fourth.

Think back for a moment and remember where you were ten years ago, or even five. I bet you're doing better than you realize. Are you still inhaling and exhaling? If so, then declare, "I am a winner!" My mother used to say, "The only losers are the ones who don't show up."

It's the tough times in life that stretch us and cause our faith muscles to grow. Like lifting weights for the body, passing the tests of life make us strong and help transform us into Christ's likeness. Come on now, one, two, three. One, two, three.

Choose to get excited about your journey with Jesus. How about waking up each day when the glorious sun rises and say out loud, "I'm excited to see how this day unfolds!" In confessing that, you can step into the day with expectation. If we're murmuring and communicating negativity, this can become a self-fulfilling prophecy.

We all sin and fall short of the glory, so let's never give up. Let's pray together and believe for the restoration God intends, realizing that sin often masks itself as our friend when in reality it will always betray us. Sin intends to kill and destroy, and it always takes us further than we want to go and keeps us longer than we want to stay. Take note: The Lord will set you free from your enemies, not from your friends.

If you are in need of restoration, I want to encourage you.

God's River of Restoration can flow into your life. Places that were once damaged, ruined, and dry can spring to life. Invite God in today.

SPRINGBOARDS TO HELP YOU
JUMP INTO THE RIVER

1. **Put God first.** The River of Restoration comes from God. As you put Him first in your heart, your life will be filled with everything you need. "Seek first His kingdom and His righteousness, and all these things will be added to you" (Matthew 6:33).

2. **Worship.** Worshiping God makes a way for the River to flow into your heart and life. At one point during my life crisis all I could do was whisper, "Alleluia." I know that was divinely inspired and I know it was enough to bring me out of a pit. As Ruth Ward Heflin said, "Praise the Lord until the worship comes. Worship the Lord until the glory comes. Then, stand in the glory." Oh my, everything is eclipsed by the glory of God.

3. **Fellowship.** Spend time with those who believe in the fullness of God's power and love. Fellowship with other believers offers encouragement, focus and empowerment.

CHAPTER TWO

The Journey

IN THE BEGINNING

Let's start this restoration journey in the beginning; it seems logical, right? We see in Genesis 1:31 that when God created everything, He said it was "very good." We have an excellent reason right there to believe in restoration of the good things of God. Certainly, the Creator of the Universe does not want any part of His good creation stolen or destroyed – that's why He restores. It's true that sin causes destruction but it's also true that Jesus came to fulfill God's plan of redemption. Redemption includes salvation, of course, but it also includes *restoration from the devastation* caused by sin. Even though the thief has ployed to steal, kill and destroy ever since that first encounter with Adam and Eve, Jesus came to restore it all and give us an abundant life (John 10:10).

When we surrender our lives to God, restoration begins on a very personal level. The Spirit of God redeems and restores our bodies, souls and spirits. Restoration is continuous; it never stops until eternity. Philippians 1:6 says it like this, "He who began a good work in you will perfect it until the day of Christ Jesus."

On this journey of restoration, the Holy Spirit does what only He can do, while you actively engage. Following are some fundamentals of your engagement:

GRAB HOLD OF THAT MANUAL!

Everything in our life is not restored immediately; it's a process, so don't jump off the potter's wheel. I like to explain the process as follows: When you walk up to an altar in a church, or you're on your knees in your bedroom, or perhaps even in a foxhole in a war zone, no matter where you surrender your life to God, at that moment you are redeemed. Boom! But let's say at that moment of supernatural redemption, as you're filled with the spirit of God, you do not know how to cook. Guess what? You still will not know how to cook. You'll need to be diligent and study a recipe book for that knowledge. It's that same way with restoration and the Bible, which is our guide to experiencing a fulfilled, restored life. Be diligent, find a Bible translation that you enjoy, and begin to learn God's promises so you can step into them and take responsibility for your role in the restoration process.

As we walk with the Lord we learn that His Word is alive, living and sharper than a double-edged sword. Don't skim over the words; make the Scriptures your own and truly believe that they are alive and active. In other words, the Bible is not just ink on paper. It is the supernatural, inspired Word of God waiting for you to speak it – to send it out so it can accomplish God's promises (Isaiah 55:11). Listen, the angels do God's bidding and they're waiting to hear your voice (Psalm 103:20).

CO-LABOR WITH GOD

We can't just sit in a chair and expect a magical restoration pill to drop into our mouth. Rather, we co-labor with God to that end, cooperating with Holy Spirit, the Helper. We learn to hear the voice of our Shepherd as He teaches us about good vs. evil and about restoration vs. destruction – and then we act accordingly.

For example, it seems ridiculous to expect God to restore a person's health if they are consistently filling their body with toxins. Putting alcohol, drugs, nicotine or unhealthy foods into a human body, all the while praying for restored health, is not co-laboring with God. Quite the opposite, in fact; poisons can produce premature death. Addiction demons are from the evil one who comes to destroy – he has an assignment on your life. Freedom is from the Lord who comes to give restoration and abundant life.

Likewise, why would we expect God to provide restoration of finances if we grossly overspend and go deep into debt? That would be foolish, and God is wisdom. However, when Holy Spirit lovingly reveals troubling areas in our lives that we may have created due to poor choices, we turn from those ways and turn towards God. He is a loving teacher and shows us the way to abundant life. Father knows best.

SOW ... THEN REAP

For many years of my life I didn't have a nice bed. Even as a child, that was something the enemy used as a trigger to upset me. In fact, one of my dreams is to start a cause that would be called, "A Bed for Every Child." Every child in the world deserves a warm, safe place to rest and be restored.

When I learned how to break free from a spirit of poverty and live under the undeniable Kingdom principle that says we reap what we sow, I simply started sowing with what I had – often small things. Even with offerings, Holy Spirit would whisper, "Always give something." So, if that meant quietly laying nickels and pennies in the offering plate, I did it. I am thrilled to boast in the Lord and testify that, since sowing for many years, I have had the honor of giving away several complete bedroom suites. They just seem to keep multiplying – smile. Thank You, Jesus.

I once had a car that needed some serious restoration. For many years I drove that old car and it was like the Israelites' sandals, it just didn't wear out. I prayed and believed that a new car was on the way and frequently said, "I'm just driving this old car until God brings my Lexus." I was half joking and wholly prophesying, hardly realizing the power of declarations and calling things that are not as though they are (Romans 4:17). The old car ran okay, but the battery had major problems. I can't even count how many times I went on ministry trips only to return to my garage and find the car battery dead. I spent a small fortune having mechanics look for the cause of the battery drain.

One day, a couple I'd only met two or three times pulled into my driveway and gifted me with a beautiful pearl white Lexus. They handed me the keys and the title. As my knees buckled, I understood Deuteronomy 28:2 for the first time, where God says His blessings will overtake us. It was months later when I remembered I had at one time given an old car away. Oh my gosh! I had sowed a car. We serve the God of upgrades. That gift from the Lord changed my life and I know He wants to change yours. Our heavenly Bridegroom loves to give gifts to His Bride.

I know hundreds of people who share their testimonies of how

God turned their lives around and RESTORED what had been stolen! What tests are becoming your testimony? Surrender to God, co-labor with Him and watch your mess become a miracle. What the enemy means for harm, God can use for good (Genesis 50:20).

WORK THE WORD

The Word of God is power. Thousands of years ago God said, "Let there be light." There was and still is light. His words remain powerful and eternal and He chooses you to read them, believe them, and declare them. Our Heavenly Father's living Word can transform and restore us, touching every area of our lives, if we let it. In other words, God's Word works if we work it.

Here are a few ways to work the Word:

Believe – It's crucial to believe in the Word of God. "For this reason we also constantly thank God that when you received the word of God which you heard from us, you accepted it not as the word of men, but for what it really is, the word of God, which also performs its work in you who believe" (1 Thessalonians 2:13).

Search – Search the Word for the Scriptures that you need. Holy Spirit will help you and illuminate them to you. Memorize them and declare them.

Have Faith – We walk by faith and not by sight. Faith comes first; it is a choice. God will do what He says He will do!

Pray the Scriptures – When you find the appropriate Scriptures for your situation, pray them. God listens and fulfills His Word.

Give Thanks – Give God thanks for His Word and His promises. This proves to Him that you believe His Word, and that pleases Him.

Meditate – Hebrews 4:12 (NKJV) tells us that God's work is "living and powerful." So it is important to let it soak into our hearts and minds. It is a sword that cuts through our conscience, never enabling, always empowering.

Declare – Isaiah 55:11 promises that if we speak and declare the promises of God, those words cannot return empty; they must accomplish what they are sent out to do.

Do It! – Jesus was about His Father's business and so are we. When Holy Spirit illuminates Scriptures to you, ask yourself what the life application is. We want to be doers of the Word, not just hearers.

GLORY NEVER GOES BACKWARDS

As believers in Jesus, who is the Restorer, we can be set free from strongholds in life that hold us back; we always want to be marching *forward*. It is with great delight that we learn to long for God's destiny for us to be fulfilled. We learn to stay alert and to be cautious not to return to any type of slavery, or to willfully sin. If we get lax about our spiritual walk with the Lord and don't stay in His living Word, it is possible to slip back into bondages.

Let's say for instance that someone struggles with an addiction. They know better and realize that Christians are supposed to take good care of their bodies, temples of the Holy Spirit, but it's still a struggle. So, they purpose to consistently *fight the good fight of faith* and serve One True God; no idols allowed! They make a calculated decision not to take one step backward because it is finished; where the Spirit of the Lord is, there is freedom – period.

Listen, God's glory never goes backwards. Ponder on this amazing Scripture for a moment:

We can all draw close to him with the veil removed from our faces. And with no veil we all become like mirrors who brightly reflect the glory of the Lord *Jesus*. We *are* being transfigured into his very image as we move from one brighter level of glory to another. And this glorious transfiguration comes from the Lord, who is the Spirit.

– 2 Corinthians 3:18 (TPT)

Alleluia! The Lord transforms us as we go from one level of glory to another level of glory, restoring us to His likeness. Just think, that has been His goal ever since He created mankind – you – in His image. With the Lord, each struggle, every challenge, can be an opportunity to be transformed, strengthened and restored. Step forward – We all have free will, the power of choice to do so.

Try thinking of your Christian journey, walking hand-in-hand with Jesus, as you climb a ladder to heaven. We're only here on earth for a short period of time, relative to eternity. In fact, James 4:14 says we're just a mist of vapor that appears for a little while and then vanishes. So, let's stay focused on the ultimate goal of eternity, realizing that we're spiritual beings with a short human experience.

God's plan of Redemption/restoration is designed to transform us. Each time we pass a love test, each time we come through a storm in our lives, we continue to walk with Jesus to the next level of glory ... *after* we pass the test with grace and love. If we don't pass it, not to worry, we get lots of do-overs.

JACOB'S LADDER

Remember the song, "We Are Climbing Jacob's Ladder"? I used to sing it a lot as a child. It goes like this:

We are climbing Jacob's ladder
We are climbing Jacob's ladder
We are climbing Jacob's ladder
Soldiers of the Cross.

Every rung goes higher and higher
Every rung goes higher and higher
Every rung goes higher and higher
Soldiers of the Cross.

Now, that might sound silly to some, but it creates a great visual aid, showing how we can go from glory to glory, eventually reaching our eternal destination – heaven.

A PLACE CALLED HEAVEN

Of course, the song depicts Genesis 28 where God gives Jacob a vision and promises to bless him even while Jacob was using a stone as a pillow. Despite his hard, natural surroundings, Jacob totally trusted a supernatural God, and in doing so he was shown the conduit between heaven and earth. When Jacob awoke from his sleep, he said, "Surely the Lord is in this place, and I did not know it." He was afraid and said, "How awesome is this place! This is none other than the house of God, *and this is the gate of heaven*" (Genesis 28:16-17).

We too, might feel like we're surrounded by hard circumstances, seeking rest when it seems like our pillow is a stone. But it's time to awake and rise up, knowing there is a much better place awaiting us; a place that is awesome. A place called heaven where the streets are paved with gold and there is no pain and no sorrow; the perfection of paradise, RESTORED. God's spiritual ladder helps us stay focused as we access it and go higher with Him until one day we see Him face to face.

In Acts 3:21 we see that it says, "Whom the heaven must receive until the time of the restoration of all things; which God has spoken by the mouth of all His prophets since the world began."

So Jesus returned to heaven following His death and resurrection, and in due time God will restore all things; everything created by God will be restored. All promises to Israel – restored. Godly things in heaven and on earth will be restored. This will be the dispensation of the fullness of time (Ephesians 1:10).

Oh my, isn't it exciting to know that God's restoration has begun and you're a part of it? Don't miss out! Find out what the Lord is doing on earth and join Him, friend. And, as restoration takes place in you and in your life, remember that your ultimate destiny is not temporal but eternal. We live our lives in peace, focused and about Father's business.

LET'S DECLARE:

1. I am climbing Jacob's ladder and surely the Lord is in this place.
2. I am going from glory to glory.
3. God is restoring me and many aspects of the Kingdom of God before Jesus returns.
4. I am making myself ready.
5. I am the righteousness of Christ.
6. I am filled with the same spirit that raised Christ from the dead.
7. Resurrection power restores abundant life.
8. I will worship my King – *Alleluia.*

CHAPTER THREE

Believe, Blessed, Beauty

ONLY BELIEVE

In order to prepare for and believe in restoration, it is crucial to believe that God Himself is love, and also believe what He has promised us as a result of that love. He loves you so much that He sent His only Son just for you so that the curse would be reversed – even to the degree that you should not perish but have everlasting life. There's eternal restoration right there. We get a better understanding of what everlasting life looks like in John 10:10: God teaches us that the enemy comes to steal, kill and destroy, but Jesus came to give us – rather, restore us to – *abundant life*.

In the Garden of Eden, God filled Adam and Eve's life with abundance and goodness. However, He told Adam and Eve that if they ate from the tree of the knowledge of good and evil they would die (Genesis 2:17). But the father of lies, disguised as a serpent, told Eve that God was the liar. In fact, the devil said that they would not die but would become like God (Genesis 3:4–5). To the world's demise, Adam and Eve believed the lie.

Are you getting this? As long as Adam and Eve believed God, they had abundant life. But when they were deceived by the deceiver, and believed the lie, paradise as they knew it was replaced with misery. Sin had temporarily won, and so began the fall of man for Adam, Eve and each one of us. At that time, God spoke a curse, inherited by all (Genesis 3:17–19). But wait! God had a perfect plan for restitution – He sent His Son who said, "I am the resurrection and the life." We could paraphrase this as Jesus saying, "I have come to reverse the curse" or, "I have come to bring life, not death; restoration, not destruction."

In 1 Corinthians 15:22 we see restoration at its finest. "For as in Adam all die, so also in Christ *all shall be made alive*" (NKJV). How marvelous! Jesus reverses the curse for all who will believe in Him, and in His promises God had a plan for perfect redemption; Jesus came to restore.

SHALOM

The Hebrew word for "restoration" comes from the same root word as *shalom*. In English we think of *shalom* as peace, and that is correct. But there's more. At its Hebrew core, *peace* means "nothing missing, nothing broken." Shalom comes from *shalem*, a verb, an action word, meaning "to restore, to make whole," which means that God makes us whole.

There is no English word that can accurately convey the richness of the word *shalom*. *Strong's Concordance* defines its many meanings.

H7965 – *shalowm shä·lōm'* – peace, well, peaceably, welfare, salute, prosperity, safe, health, peaceable

H7999 – *shalam shä·lam'* – pay, peace, recompense, reward, render, restore, repay, perform, good, end, requite, restitution, finished, again, amends, full

Shalom and its related words, *Shalem, Shelem* and their

derivatives, are very important theological words in the Old Testament. *Shalom* occurs over 250 times in 213 separate verses. The KJV translates 172 of these as "peace."

THE FUTURE IS NOW

In the Old Testament we hear the Word of God prophesying future restoration: "For unto us a Child is born, unto us a Son is given; and the government will be upon His shoulder. And His name will be called Wonderful, Counselor, Mighty God, Everlasting Father, Prince of Peace (*shalowm*)" (Isaiah 9:6 NKJV). Based on our word study above, we could replace the word "peace" here with "restore" and say, "The Lord is the Prince of Restoration."

> "The Lord bless you and keep you; The Lord make His face shine upon you, and be gracious to you; The Lord lift up His countenance upon you, And give you peace (*shalowm*)."
> – Numbers 6:24-26 (NKJV)

Again, we could say, "The Lord lift up His countenance upon you, and give you *restoration*."

> "For I know the thoughts that I think toward you, says the Lord, thoughts of peace (*shalowm*) and not of evil, to give you a future and a hope." – Jeremiah 29:11 (NKJV)

In other words: Thoughts of restoration, completeness, wholeness, nothing missing, nothing broken.

Here is a great illustration of how, in verb form, it is translated as "restore":

> "I will restore (*shalam*) to you the years that the locust hath eaten, the cankerworm, and the caterpillar, and the palmerworm…" – Joel 2:25 (KJV)

35

The concept of flourishing, restoration, or *shalom* continues in the New Testament, where writers translated *shalom* as the Greek word *Eirene*, "Peace." They embraced the Old Testament concept of *shalom* so the world would see the good news Jesus preached as the gospel of *shalom* (Acts 10:36; Ephesians 2:17, 6:15). We are called to aim toward *shalom* and the Kingdom of God. "Blessed are the peacemakers, for they shall be called sons of God" (Matthew 5:9).

BLESSED ARE THE SHALOM-MAKERS

In Greek, the word for "peacemaker" is *eirhnopoioi* – literally, a founder or promoter of peace. And in Hebrew, the word for "peace" is, of course, *shalom*.

Now that we understand the meaning of *shalom*, we can understand the whole meaning of peacemaker. "Peace," or *shalom*, does not just mean the absence of war or harmonious relationships. It is your entire well-being. When we are well and whole, *we live a lifestyle of shalom as we help restore abundant life to others* – not by accident but by divine assignment. May your sphere of influence be radiant with *shalom*, because that's who God intends you to be.

Jesus didn't say, "Blessed are peace keepers," or "Blessed are those who have peace." He said, "Blessed are the peacemakers." Isn't it wonderful to know that God sent His Son to bring peace on earth? So that we could choose to make peace with God, He first made peace with us. We learn to make peace with ourselves and with others. Again, restoration/wholeness is a process. We cannot give out what is not in us.

Bottom line: When God **restores** you, you can become a **restorer**, and that leads to an abundant life, because God said, "Blessed are the shalom-makers!" Get it? Oh, how He wants to bless you.

Romans 14:19 is a beautiful Scripture: "We pursue the things which make for peace and the building up of one another."

And 2 Corinthians 13:11 kind of sums up life: "Finally, brothers and sisters, rejoice! Strive for full restoration, encourage one another, be of one mind, live in peace. And the God of love and peace will be with you" (NIV).

The earth needs more peacemakers, more restorers, as God's Kingdom comes to earth as it is in heaven. If you're not already, you are now on your way to becoming a peace-builder, a shalom-maker!

WHAT DOES A SHALOM-MAKER DO?

Shalom-makers bring good news and comfort to the brokenhearted.

Shalom-makers are people of action; love is a verb.

Shalom-makers become a safe harbor for others to share their hearts with, despite differences; all are welcome, all are honored.

Shalom-makers look for strengths, not weaknesses, first in themselves and then in others.

Shalom-makers always empower and never enable.

Shalom-makers forgive quickly and facilitate reconciliation.

Shalom-makers listen to hearts, not just words.

Shalom-makers restore and help make whole, looking at the present lack of peace and searching for the root of dissension.

Shalom-makers consistently grow in the fruit of the Spirit: Love, joy, peace, patience, kindness, goodness, faithfulness (Galatians 5:22).

Shalom-makers emerge out of meekness, quiet inner strength.

Shalom-makers express God's character and shall be called the sons of God.

As you move forward from glory to glory, be sure you become a peacemaker and not a peacekeeper. A peacekeeper tends to walk on eggshells because they never want to upset anyone or anything. They try to avoid conflict which, of course, is impossible in this world. Conflict resolution, on the other hand, is a beautiful thing. Peacekeepers often operate out of fear, hiding their true feelings, which can make them vulnerable to abusive ways, whereas peacemakers restore out of strength and God-confidence.

Our Heavenly Father sent His only Son to bring peace and goodwill to mankind, so when we are peacemakers we are like our Father. As you arise and shine, ask the Lord where you are called to be a shalom-maker, spreading the DNA of God. Perhaps in a business, an orphanage, a school. Wherever it is, it's a glorious plan. Once we are made whole by our God, we are sent to help make others whole – shalom. I believe that as more peacemakers emerge, fewer peacekeepers will exist.

"LORD, I WANT TO BE RESTORED!"

We have seen how *shalom* – simply translated as "peace" in most of our versions, comes from a root meaning "to restore, to be made whole." It is up to each of us to decide if we want to go through this process to become not only receivers, but eventually shalom keepers, too. Like our brother in the gospel of Mark, we can choose to step forward – we can say, "Lord, I want to be restored!" Mark 3:3-5, goes on: "He [Jesus] said to the man who had the withered hand, 'Step forward.' Then He said to them, 'Is it lawful on the Sabbath to do good or to do evil, to save life or to kill?' But they kept silent. And when He had looked around at them with anger, being grieved by the hardness of their hearts, He said to the man, 'Stretch out your hand.' And he stretched it out, and his hand was restored as whole as the other."

Jesus made him whole – surely not only his hand, but everything within him spiritually, emotionally and mentally – as a result of dealing with his physical ailment. What about you? I encourage you to embrace restoration – shalom – today!

BEAUTY FOR ASHES

To console those who mourn in Zion, to give them beauty for ashes, the oil of joy for mourning, the garment of praise for the spirit of heaviness; that they may be called trees of righteousness, the planting of the Lord, that He may be glorified.   – Isaiah 61:3

Beauty here refers to a bridal crown. Wood ashes placed upon the head expressed mourning, but a nuptial garland signified gladness. The symbolism in this Scripture depicts festive joy as part of the reign of Jesus Christ. The spirit of heaviness refers to discouragement. It is to be replaced by abundant life (the garment of praise).

How exciting to know that God says He can give us beauty for ashes! Let's note the divine exchange that takes place in Isaiah 61:3. Surely we all want beauty, but we need to give God our ashes to get it. Sometimes people unknowingly hold onto their ashes. Sorrow becomes comfortable to them and yet they can't understand why they are not seeing restoration. Have you ever had a wound, let's say, on your arm, and as it heals it feels good to gently rub the wound and nurture it? This is similar to what can happen when wounds of the soul aren't healed properly and we aren't aware of the devil's tactics. The enemy likes to continously bring up the incident, the trauma, that caused the wound, and then our mind automatically begins to nurture that old wound by recalling the drama, *until* we recognize what's happening, let go, and let God. With the renewing of our mind we learn that by giving the ashes of our past to God, He restores and gives us beauty for the future.

Ashes can be wounded areas in our souls, our businesses, our marriages and so on. No one is without wounds ... without ashes. It's how we choose to handle the ashes of life that allows the Creator to make something beautiful.

Maybe you are even suffering the consequences of self-inflicted wounds and need to forgive yourself.

KEYS TO EXCHANGING ASHES FOR BEAUTY:

- Try to see yourself from God's perspective. Oh, how He loves you!

- Rejoice in God's amazing forgiveness, as far as the east is from the west (Psalm 103:12).

- Remember that you are never condemned or rejected by God. He Himself has said, "I will never leave you nor forsake you." – Hebrews 13:5 (NKJV)

- Get rid of the negative thoughts about yourself and replace them with positive ones.

- Ask yourself if you are just repeating what God says in the Bible, or are you learning to truly hear Him and respond to His truth?

- Let go of pain and bitterness. The Lord will help you with this as you talk with Him about it. He wants you restored, whole and full of joy.

- Let go of offenses – they won't let go of you. We choose what we take on.

- Practice saying, "I am the righteousness of Christ" (see 2 Corinthians 5:21)

- Embrace the word that says, "The voice of a stranger I will not hear" (see John 10:5).

- Learn to listen and follow the voice of the one true God (see John10:27).

- Learn to take every thought captive (2 Corinthians 10:5).

CHAPTER FOUR

The Second Half of Life Is Better than the First

LATTER DAYS

Now the Lord blessed the latter days of Job more than his beginning; for he had fourteen thousand sheep, six thousand camels, one thousand yoke of oxen, and one thousand female donkeys.
                                                          – Job 42:12

Too often, those who are in the second half of life look back at the first half (or maybe the first two thirds) and have regrets. Regrets may be from personal choices or even circumstances not always in their control, with disappointing, difficult outcomes. Ironically, sometimes the regrets are for an opposite reason – those earlier years were full of life, fruit and fulfillment, and now there is a feeling of loss.

No matter how you may look at the ashes of years past, I have great news ... there is restoration ... the second half of life (or even the final third!) can be better than the first.

JUST SAY "YES"

One key to enjoying restoration and the second half of life is to say "yes." "Yes, I choose to walk in peace that passes all human understanding. Yes, I will set my sights on the eternal purposes of God and contribute to the world. Yes, I *will* leave a legacy. Yes, I will walk in passion and purpose for Christ, who gave His passionate love for me." When Rick Warren wrote *The Purpose Driven Life*, he sold over 20 million copies in the first two years. People are looking for purpose because without purpose/vision people perish (see Proverbs 29:18 KJV).

Another key is *believing* that God *can* and *will* restore, so that the second half of our lives will be better than the first. Luke 8:50 NIV teaches us to "just believe."

And pay attention to what Peter says in Acts 10:34 (NLT): "I see very clearly that God shows no favoritism." So God will do for us as He did for our brother Job.

Lastly, it's important to finish up the first half of life strongly. Realize that all things work together for good for those who love God and are called according to His purpose (see Romans 8:28). Tie up that first half of life with a tidy little bow and head into the future!

What if you make a conscious decision right now and write a declaration saying: "This is going to be the best year of my life!" There you go! Sometimes we pray and wait on God when really, He's waiting on us. He's already promised us abundant life, so let's go after it. Be ready to co-labor with God in this endeavor. What people, places and things need to remain in your life? What needs to go? Are there things on your bucket list that you've put off for many years? If so, what are you waiting for? Perhaps now is the time to believe and receive.

SENIOR AMBASSADORS

I want to take time here to honor Senior Ambassadors – those who are 60 and over. What an honor to co-labor with the Lord as He releases an army of Senior Ambassadors to do great exploits. I'm thrilled to be part of a multigenerational move of God where seniors support millennials and undergird their visions, while millennials honor seniors and draw from their wisdom. God wants His entire army mobilized – men, women and children. It's so exciting to create the prototype and build this worldwide movement.

The Lord has been showing me that it is crucial that the end-time army *gets ready and stays ready*. As God manifests signs, wonders and miracles on the earth, we will see restoration, revival and reformation at unprecedented levels. We will see a great harvest of souls larger than mankind has ever known; millions of people will be coming to know the Lord. Jesus is not willing that any should perish, and He is calling you to serve in the army of God to co-labor in this great harvest. It is our responsibility to be certain God's army isn't broken and wounded, just hobbling along, barely getting by. We must rise up, marching on the frontlines, believing that, "as our days are, so our strength will be" (see Deuteronomy 33:25). There are wonderful, amazing assignments arriving from heaven, and restoration is key to them being accomplished.

TIME FOR THOSE "DRY BONES" TO REVIVE

In Ezekiel 37, the army of God is not ready until the spirit of God takes action and breathes on the dry bones, bringing dead things to life. Let's take note of verse 11 in this vision that God gives Ezekiel. "Our bones are dry, our hope is lost, and we ourselves are cut off!" (NKJV) It sounds like restoration is greatly needed, right?

To put it another way, in Ezekiel's vision God shows him an entire army whose passion has disappeared, both passion for their God and passion for their destinies. These people had lost their hope and they were cut off, separated and divided from abundant life. This army felt all washed up; they were so done. They truly needed hope renewed. So, the question is, "How are they going to be revived ... filled with life?" Well, verses 4 and 5 say that God sends a prophet to prophesy to the dry bones and THEN He breathes into them so they shall live and not die.

Read verse 14, " 'I will put My Spirit in you, and you shall live, and I will place you in your own land. Then you shall know that I, the Lord, have spoken it and performed it,' says the Lord."

Are there dry bones in your life that need to be revived? If so, the Lord clearly shows us three ingredients for personal and corporate revival:

1. **PRESENCE OF GOD** – His Spirit will be in YOU and you shall live!

2. **POWER OF GOD'S LIVING WORD** – "Again He said to me, 'Prophesy to these bones, and say to them, "O dry bones, hear the word of the Lord!"'" (verse 4)

3. **PROMISES OF GOD** – " 'I will put My Spirit in you, and you shall live, and I will place you in your own land. Then you shall know that I, the Lord, have spoken it and performed it," says the Lord.'" (verse 14)

Right now, right where you are, read the words of the Lord out loud and prophesy over yourself. Remember, God's words are alive, they are active, and must accomplish what you send them to do. God will indeed restore you; He will make you whole.

Hebrews 13:20-21 (NKJV) talks about God's wholeness: "May the God of peace … through the blood of the everlasting covenant … make you complete (*katartizo*) in every good work to do His will, working in you what is well pleasing in His sight, through Jesus Christ, to whom be glory forever."

No matter how many self-help books we read, or how many counselors we meet with, it's God, the Creator of the Universe, who makes us whole. He makes us complete, so we can fulfill our purpose in life.

Now, the word *complete* in Hebrews 13 does not mean "finished." According to Strong's Concordance, the Greek word for "complete" is *katertizo* (kat-ar-ti'-zo). *Kataretizo* means repairing what has been broken, restoring what's damaged, and reconciling what has been torn apart, or re-equipping us for a continual process of wholeness. Do you want to be re-equipped? God is speaking to all people, but in this season, I hear Him calling out Seniors and saying, "GET READY, STAY READY, as I prepare my end-time army."

The Lord is very aware that you have been through some tough stuff. He is omniscient; He knows all and hears all! Listen to this exciting word in Genesis 50:20, "You meant evil against me, but God meant it for good in order to bring about this present result." That's our God, working all things together for good. This Scripture is Joseph speaking after being sold into slavery by jealous brothers, thrown into prison on false charges, and overcoming many other humongous clashes. Yet, after all the challenges he faced, Joseph remained free of bitterness or regret. He still loved and trusted God even in the worst of circumstances. Many years after his brothers had thrown him in a pit to die, he speaks to them face to face and graciously says, "You meant it for bad; God meant it for good."

GUARD YOUR HEART

As you are restored, I want to encourage you to make wise choices along the way. God can take what the enemy meant for harm and turn it into a blessing, if we choose to become better and not bitter. God is not looking for a wimpy, beat up army. He's looking for overcomers who do great exploits for their King!

During some hurricanes in the USA, I prayed and watched the news coverage closely, since I had family members living in the path of the storms. Some of these hurricanes were huge – historical. As I talked on the phone with my sister and niece, who were making the long trek north out of Florida to North Carolina, they were amazed at the thousands of cars traveling bumper to bumper even at 3:30 a.m. You see, most Floridians have been trained on safety when it comes to hurricanes. They have storm shutters ready to put on the windows of their homes, extra food and gasoline stored away, and a plan to head to safety if evacuations are necessary. I repeat, they have a plan.

I wonder how many of us are always prepared for the storms of life. This is such a crucial part of our walk with the Lord, as often there's not much time to get ready when a storm is imminent. Have we hidden the Word of God in our heart so it brings constant strength as the winds of life howl? Do we have storm shutters ready to guard our hearts? We should, since our hearts are the wellspring of life (Proverbs 4:23). I'm not talking about putting up walls that prevent love from coming in and going out. I'm talking about guarding. We must always have our armor of steel on the outside but remain soft, gentle and kind on the inside. Get ready, stay ready.

WAYS TO MAKE WISE CHOICES

- We choose to lean into the peace of God that passes all human understanding (Philippians 4:7).

- We choose to be transformed into Christ's likeness and get better, not bitter.

- We choose not to be prisoners of our past, knowing the past was a lesson, not a prison sentence.

- We choose to forgive quickly and ask God to help us forget.

- We choose to re-fire and not retire.

- We choose not to jump off the potter's wheel even when the molding seems intense.

- We choose to step into the Living Word, knowing that all things work together for good.

- We choose to draw a line in the sand and say, "No more unhealthy grieving, unhealthy eating, etc. No more! I am moving forward ... restored, made whole."

- We choose to keep our eyes on the Healer and not on the pain.

- We choose to worship the King of Kings, knowing it's the highest form of warfare.

- We choose to give God our battles because they belong to Him (2 Chronicles 20:15).

CHAPTER FIVE

New Wineskins

OLD WINESKINS RESTORED

Nor do they put new wine into old wineskins, or else the wineskins break, the wine is spilled, and the wineskins are ruined. But they put new wine into new wineskins, and both are preserved.   – Matthew 9:17

If new wine is poured into old wineskins, as the new wine ferments (gets sweeter with age) it causes pressure. This causes the old wineskin to burst and both the old wineskin and the new wine are lost – all is lost. We cannot put new ideas into old mindsets. We cannot get new results with old behaviors.

Historically, old wineskins were not thrown away. They were RESTORED, in other words, they were made "new" again. The skins were turned inside-out (ouch), then they were scraped clean with a knife (kind of like a two-edged sword) and oiled (like anointing oil – James 5:14), so they were soft and pliable.

New wineskins have the ability to expand and be stretched. They can broaden. Are we willing to expand at any age, even when it's uncomfortable? Stretching is usually uncomfortable but so necessary to make place for the new:

SOME WAYS WE ARE STRETCHED

1. Learning and preparing for new assignments

I love to learn. I feel like if I'm not learning/growing, I'm dying. In fact, as soon as I finish an assignment from heaven, I'm already asking the Lord for my next one. It's an amazing, exciting way to live.

I'm sure you've experienced (or heard of) little children standing on something, like the arm of a couch, and jumping into their father's arms. The child is totally trusting their earthly father; in fact, they are filled with excitement and delight. The moment they jump into the arms of their father, by faith, believing that the outcome will be grand, what do they say? "Do it again, daddy, do it again!" We should be the same way with our Heavenly Father. We're about our Father's business and when we finish an assignment let's be ready to jump into our Maker's arms with wild abandon, saying, "Do it again, Abba. Do it again!"

Don't let a fall or a disappointment rob you from the desires of your heart. Your Father will pick you up and restore what's been broken. Because He put those desires in your heart, He wants them fulfilled even more than you do. Ready, set? Now get up, stand tall, and jump.

2. Replacing destructive patterns

We are all products of a set of behaviors and concepts. It's very important to realize that fact and own it. Then, adopt God's TRUTH. Ask yourself today, what needs to "change" from glory to glory in your life?

When we break out of old ways, we break through into new levels of restoration. Restoration is perpetual and brings about upgrades, but we must reach for it – step into it. Let's be careful not to try to pull God down to our level. Let's reach up for His image, as we were created in His image.

If you haven't already, today is a good day to replace old, destructive patterns with new healthy ones. We're never too young or too old to change, friend. Make lifestyle changes – not just temporary ones but permanent ones. As we replace old wineskins (patterns) with new wineskins (patterns) we are transformed. Oh, my goodness! How thrilling is that? "We all, with unveiled face, *continually* seeing as in a mirror the glory of the Lord, are *progressively* being transformed into His image from [one degree of] glory to [even more] glory, which comes from the Lord, [who is] the Spirit" (2 Corinthians 3:18 AMP).

Take some time to pray and ask God to set you free from hardened, brittle wineskins that can break easily. We don't want all to be lost.

Remember, old wineskins are not discarded, they are made new! God is looking for those who are "new wineskins." They have been emptied of the old, cleansed and restored. They are ready to be expanded with the new wine. As vessels of the Lord they long to be filled with the fullness of Christ and live for His purposes. They long to be filled with the fruit and the power of God.

When Jesus brought the Gospel of the Kingdom, it did not fit into pharisaical paradigms because they adhered to the inflexible legalism of the old covenant. The Lord brings a new way of living. Still today, apostles continue to teach the Gospel of the Kingdom and we must apply the new wine concept, the new way of living, to our own lives.

IDENTIFYING OLD WINESKINS

One of the first steps in turning old wineskins into new ones is to identify them and ask Holy Spirit for help. He is the Helper, the Paraclete. Perhaps write down some old wineskins in your own life that you believe the Lord would like to make new. Make notes, or at least a mental note, as they pop up in your life.

What would some old wineskins be? These are some that immediately come to my mind. Surely you can think of others.

Wrong doings – Perhaps after many years you still cheat on your taxes, just a tiny bit, of course, while God is saying, "I want to bless you more but I need a new, pure wineskin to pour the blessing into."

Worship preferences – We also must be careful not to get stuck in old religious systems when God is saying, "I am doing a new thing." Of course, the gospel will always be perfect and timeless, but the new wine flows from heaven in new wineskins (packaging) with fresh ideas for all of God's people. How many millenials do you think would attend a church service, excited to worship the King, if only an 1850s pipe organ donned the choir loft? Old religious traditions can be paralyzing. The song "Amazing Grace" will never, ever lose its anointing, but in this day and age it's often played on an electric guitar. And don't say guitars and drum sets aren't for worship. Of course they are, the earth belongs to the Lord and all that is in it. God is restoring His instruments to their rightful place. He is restoring His Kingdom on earth as it is in heaven. Where the Spirit of the Lord is, there is liberty.

Old habits – I know when I am passionate about something, I tend to interrupt people. I do not like talking over others at all, it's just that I get excited and can't stop talking. Or can I? Of course, I can. Once I identified this old habit (wineskins) and took note of it, I was surprised at how often it was happening. It does happen when I'm passionate about things, but I believe it also stems from the fact that for a huge portion of my life I was to be seen and not heard.

Once we realize we all truly have a voice for truth, it takes time to temper that and learn when to speak and when to be silent (Ecclesiates 3:7). Since God reveals to heal, Holy Spirit (the Helper) and I developed a plan. Each time I interrupted someone, I would stop, apologize, and state briefly that I was working to overcome this old habit. The results have been quite successful – not perfect but quite successful.

If it helps, please know that you are not alone in your old habits. The devil is a liar and he likes to isolate people, trying to make them think they're a freak of nature. But that's simply not true. You can be certain hundreds of other people are struggling just as you are. In fact, thousands of years ago the apostle Paul wrote about the challenge in Romans 7:15-20 (AMP):

> For I do not understand my own actions [I am baffled and bewildered by them]. I do not practice what I want *to do*, but I am doing the very thing I hate [and yielding to my human nature, my worldliness – my sinful capacity]. Now if I *habitually* do what I do not want to do, [that means] I agree with the Law, *confessing* that it is good (morally excellent). So now [if that is the case, then] it is no longer I who do it [the disobedient thing which I despise], but the sin [nature] which lives in me. For I know that nothing good lives in me, that is, in my flesh [my human nature, my worldliness – my sinful capacity]. For the willingness [to do good] is present in me,

but the doing of good is not.For the good that I want to do, I do not do, but I practice the very evil that I do not want. But if I am doing the very thing I do not want to do, I am no longer the one doing it [that is, it is not me that acts], but the sin [nature] which lives in me.

Come on now, you can do it. Define and conquer!

THE CHALLENGE

How do we facilitate paradigm shifts in our lives in order to promote restoration? Galatians 5:16 implores us to walk in the Spirit so that we do not carry out the desires of the flesh. Sounds easy enough. But no matter where we're at in our walk with Jesus, let's face it – some days walking in the Spirit seems like a struggle. Other days it's as natural as breathing.

Perhaps the longer people walk without the Lord the longer it takes to crucify the flesh. The Bible tells us that when we invite the Lord into our heart and are water baptized, the "old man" is dead (Romans 6). True, of course; but sometimes that "old man" seems to keep getting up from the altar where it was sacrificed. If destructive patterns, habits, and addictions have deep roots, then we may need to take the axe to them several times.

Salvation includes deliverance, or call it freedom if that makes you more comfortable. However, when we receive freedom, we still have to do our part to break the behaviors attached to the habits we've become so familiar with.

Suppose that Mr. Somebody smoked cigarettes for twenty years. Every single day, for twenty years, he got out of bed, brewed his coffee and sat down with his addiction. When he was set free through prayer, he felt a void in his life every morning. He felt uneasy, as if something was missing ... because it was. But there's good (great, actually) news! As we're discipled by Holy Spirit, He teaches us how to fill all voids with Him. When the yoke of bondage is broken, we develop new, healthy habits to replace the destructive ones. So, rather than having a cup of coffee and a cigarette each morning, Mr. Somebody began a new habit. He now reaches for his Bible as he drinks his java. Boom! His health is being restored as well as his soul. What a great way to start each morning – facing the Lord before we face the day.

Let's be flexible new wineskins as the Lord restores and conforms us to His image. God wants us to be all things to all people. There are thousands of good things on the planet we can do. I've listed a few here to inspire you. Just do it!

- Walk
- Run
- Socialize (not social media)
- Read
- Pray
- Visit the Lonesome
- Write/Journal
- Volunteer
- Travel
- Paint
- Host a Fundraiser
- Laugh
- Sing
- Care for a Pet
- Cook
- Join/Start a Group
- Practice Healthy Coping Skills

DON'T CLAIM IT

Words are very powerful, as we see in Proverbs 18:21. They either speak life or death. Think about it. When God said, "Let there be light," not only did He create light for way back when – there is still light! Wow – now that's powerful. You might say, "Yes, but I'm not God." Well no, you're not, but if you're a believer then the same spirit that raised Christ from the dead lives in you (Romans 8:11).

With that said, let's be careful to identify the old wineskins in our lives, but don't let them become labels. It saddens me when I hear people say, "I have this disease," or "My child has this disorder." No! It's not yours, so don't take it on as a permanent fixture of life. God restores! Try learning to say, "I'm battling this disease, or that destructive habit, until I get the victory." In doing so, we're acknowledging the infirmity (God reveals to heal) but we are not owning it.

THE MIND OF CHRIST

Another way to get rid of our old mindsets is to believe and receive a new mind – the mind of Christ. The apostle Paul quotes the Old Testament, Isaiah 40:13, in the New Testament, when he declares in 1 Corinthians 2:16, "We have the mind of Christ."

When we have the mind of Christ, we know that our purposes are eternal and our focus becomes streamlined and powerful. All believers receive the mind of Christ, so our perspective is Christ's perspective. We grow to know God's will and we live to bring Him glory. We grow in love, peace and self-control as God fills us with Himself.

In 1 Corinthians 2, we find some truths regarding the mind of Christ:

1) Verse 5 teaches us that divine exchange is not about us. It reads, "Faith would not rest on the wisdom of men, but on the power of God."

2) Verse 7 says, "God's wisdom was hidden but now it is revealed to mankind [you]."

3) Verses 10-12 say that all believers have the mind of Christ. It is given to us by the Spirit of God.

4) Verse 14 helps us realize that the mind of Christ cannot be understood by those without the Spirit of God.

5) Verse 16 promises us that the mind of Christ gives us insight.

All that we need, every answer for restoration and renewing of the mind, is available to us in the Word. Surely we don't want to be like the Pharisees of old and miss the new wine that God is pouring out.

Isn't it wonderful to know that Holy Spirit dwells in us and gives us wisdom to conform to the new? Surrender.

REFLECTIONS

Make a list of GOOD things, exciting things, you will do with and for the Lord. It's a new day with new wineskins!

Chapter Six

Our Kinsman Redeemer

HE SHOWS UP TO RESTORE

"The land is not to be sold with any finality, because the land belongs to me. You're sojourners and travelers with me. So throughout all of your land inheritance, grant the right of redemption for the land. If your brother becomes so poor that he has to sell a portion of his inheritance, then his nearest kinsman redeemer is to come and redeem what his brother has sold. If a person doesn't have a kinsman redeemer, but has become rich and found sufficient means for his redemption, then let him account for the years for which it was sold, return the excess to the person to whom it was sold, and then return to his property. If he's not able to redeem it back for himself, then what he sold is to remain in the hand of the buyer until the year of jubilee. In the jubilee, it is to be returned so he may return to his property."

– Leviticus 25:23-28 (ISV)

The Kinsman Redeemer showed up to restore. In the Scripture above, we see how families in Israel were protected. Laws had been set in place stating that property was to remain in the family

61

– it was not to be given away. If a person was forced to sell their inheritance in order to survive, a kinsman was to come and buy it back so that it would stay in the family and so that the relative would no longer be poor.

JESUS IS OUR KINSMAN REDEEMER

On the cross, Jesus paid the price to become our Kinsman Redeemer. He paid our debt so that we would not lose our inheritance. Of course, our debt is a moral one, not financial. Jesus paid a price for the church, His bride, which includes you and me. God did not have to redeem His bride – because the law had been broken, He could have just distributed consequences. However, since God is love, He sent Jesus Christ to redeem (restore) our inheritance.

When we know that our Redeemer lives, we have eternal assurance of redemption and restoration. We are filled with hope (expectant joy) and we know that nothing can ever separate us from the perpetual restoration of a loving Father. Our Kinsman Redeemer, Jesus, came to set us free from poverty, to restore what the enemy has stolen to its rightful owner, and to secure justice.

KEYS TO INHERITANCE AND RESTORATION

In the book of Ruth we see the role of a kinsman redeemer in action. If you're not familiar with the story, I encourage you to read the book of Ruth to grasp it fully. So much can be learned and applied to our own lives from Ruth's experience. Let's take a look.

a. Ruth stayed close to the promises of God. She clung to Naomi. "They lifted up their voices and wept again; and Orpah kissed her mother-in-law, but Ruth *clung to her*" (Ruth 1:14).

b. To cleave to the promise takes patience. Hold on! Rest at the foot of the Cross as Ruth lay at the foot of her kinsman redeemer (3:7). Be still, at peace, and watch the Father work out the details. All the promises of God were released at the foot of the Cross.

c. Ruth stayed with the harvesters (those who reap) in the fields of Boaz (Ruth 2). Once she realized that God had her in the right place she didn't run from field to field. It's important to be in the right place at the right time so restoration can take place. It's also important to serve with those who are like-minded and want to reap a harvest for their master.

d. We cannot receive restoration, the inheritance of God, if we cling to His promises one day and reject them the next. Do not waver. "But let him ask in faith, with no doubting, for he who doubts is like a wave of the sea driven and tossed by the wind. For let not that man suppose that he will receive anything from the Lord" (James 1:6-8 NKJV).

Seek the Lord and find out if there are any adjustments you need to make in order to have your inheritance restored. Are you clinging to the promises of your heavenly Bridegroom? Believe this promise: "Delight yourself also in the Lord, and He shall give you the desires of your heart" (Psalm 37:4 NKJV).

CHAPTER SEVEN

Preventative Maintenance

LITTLE FOXES SPOIL THE VINES

Catch us the foxes, the little foxes that spoil the vines, for our vines have tender grapes.   – Song of Solomon 2:15 (NKJV)

If we don't eradicate the little foxes in our lives, they can eventually become big foxes to deal with. Foxes can be very destructive and can ruin valuable things. In our Scripture here, the Shulamite woman is saying to her fiancé that they should take some preventative measures to protect what they have. If we take excellent care of what we have, we may not need so much restoration and the Lord will give us more valuable gifts from heaven. "He who is faithful in a very little thing is faithful also in much" (Luke 16:10a).

Perhaps take some time to think and pray about little obstacles and dangers in your life that need eradicating now, so they don't grow into bigger problems. Write them down and develop a plan of action and a timeline to catch the foxes.

A STITCH IN TIME SAVES NINE

As we grow older it becomes easier to understand this proverb, "A stitch in time saves nine." We learn the hard way that things can fall apart and need a lot of restoration if not properly maintained. On one occasion I purchased a pair of pre-washed jeans. I noticed that when the factory bleached and washed them, supposedly to make them look cool, the chemicals had weakened the stitches, so the seams were pulling apart in several places. I heard Holy Spirit whisper, "A stitch in time saves nine." I hadn't heard this phrase for many years, though my grandma used to say it when I was a little girl. I quickly sewed the torn areas of the jeans, and they were just like new! Procrastination can lead to the need for restoration.

> So the workmen labored, and the repair work progressed in their hands, and they restored the house of God according to its specifications and strengthened it. – 2 Chronicles 24:13

We are all a critical part of God's restoration plan: "...the workmen labored..." Living a proactive life can help eliminate the need for huge restoration jobs later.

DON'T JUMP OFF THE POTTER'S WHEEL

We've been talking about taking care of what is ours. God does the same thing. He takes care of what is His. God created us, and He takes care of us.

Genesis 2:7 tells us that mankind was created from the clay of the earth. Then 2 Corinthians 4:7 (NIV) goes further: "We have this treasure in jars of clay to show that this all-surpassing power is from God and not from us." When we think of ourselves as beautiful jars of clay, it helps us to stay on the potter's wheel, even on those days when a part of us wants to jump off.

It's so important to trust God in the restoration process. According to this verse, we're not just jars of clay, we have a powerful treasure inside, too. How amazing! When we invite Christ into our hearts we become vessels containing "the light of the gospel that displays the glory of Christ" (2 Corinthians 4:4 NIV).

Years ago, I had a dream about signs. It was just a short one – I call them snippets. In the dream, I walked into a room where there were three signs on the wall. They were made of barnwood, color-washed in a soft green, and each one said, "Trust God, Trust God, Trust God." I sure didn't need a dream interpreter for that. Oftentimes, I can still see that gift from God in my mind's eye, right when I need it.

TAKE CARE OF THE TREASURE WITHIN

Let's look at the treasure within. It's important to build up your faith as God restores your true identity in Him and leads you to your true destiny. We can't reach the second without the first. Your treasure includes:

LIGHT: Second Corinthians 4:6 (NIV) tells us that your treasure is light. "For God, who said, 'Let light shine out of darkness,' made his light shine in our hearts to give us the light of the knowledge of God's glory displayed in the face of Christ."

POWER: Second Peter 1:3 (NASB) shows us that God wants to trust us with His power – another aspect of His treasure! "His divine power has granted to us everything pertaining to life and godliness, through the true knowledge of Him who called us by His own glory and excellence."

KNOWLEDGE: In John 14:26 (NLT) we see that we also house God's treasure of knowledge. "When the Father sends the Advocate as my representative – that is, the Holy Spirit – he will teach you everything and will remind you of everything I have told you."

ETERNITY: First Corinthians 15 tells us that our bodies – our jars of clay – will one day be resurrected and become glorified, eternal bodies.

HERE ARE A FEW WAYS TO CATCH LITTLE FOXES:

- Regular car maintenance

- Proactive healthcare – annual check-ups

- Excellent care of homes, appliances and furnaces

- Commitment renewals for marriages, relationships and businesses

- Good money management skills

- Goal setting – not just saying, "Whatever will be, will be."

- Daily devotionals and Bible study – transformation

- Accountability partners

- Emotional heath check-ups – We prosper as our souls prosper (3 John 1:2)

- Life balance – work, play, rest

- Eat right and exercise

- Laughter is good medicine (Proverbs 17:22) – lighten up

What we accept, we tolerate, what we tolerate, we enable, and what we enable, we empower. We may think that a few little foxes, a few missing stitches, or just a little sin or neglect is okay. It is not. "A little leaven [a slight inclination to error, or a few false teachers] leavens the whole batch [it perverts the concept of faith and misleads the church]" (Galatians 5:9 AMP). However, it is so wonderful to have a merciful, loving Father who helps us learn life skills so we can live abundant lives. As for those seasons when we may not have managed well and where situations that were out of our control caused destruction, God can restore those years! He promised, "I will restore to you the years that the swarming locust has eaten" (Joel 2:25 NKJV).

CHAPTER EIGHT

Restoring Relationships

OUR DIVINE ROLE MODEL

We know that discipleship is following Jesus, but there's more. In John 15:15 (NKJV), Jesus tells us that the real goal of discipleship is to produce friends. "No longer do I call you servants, for a servant does not know what his master is doing; but I have called you friends, for all things that I heard from My Father I have made known to you."

Here are some important aspects of both restoring and maintaining healthy relationships.

FAITHFULNESS

"When the Son of Man comes, will He really find faith on the earth?" (Luke 18:8b NKJV). Now, I don't know about you, but I want Christ to find faith in me when He returns. I want to hear those words, "Well done, good and faithful servant," as seen in Matthew 25:21 (NIV). In hopes of hearing those words from the God that we love, it's important to maintain – and restore, if necessary – relationships with people.

First John 4:20 (NLT) makes that very clear. It reads, "If someone says, 'I love God,' but hates a fellow believer, that person is a liar; for if we don't love people we can see, how can we love God, whom we cannot see?"

Faith is foundational for Christianity, and that includes being faithful in relationships. Jesus is the perfect example of someone being faithful. He was sent to seek and save the lost and He was, and still is, faithful, even unto death. His mission, as ours, is eternal, not temporal, and He fulfilled it totally.

In our relationship with Jesus, our faith is action; we put our faith in someone. As that relationship grows and is strengthened, we have even more faith in Jesus because we experience His faithfulness while seeing His promise of restoration fulfilled in our lives. And so it is with our earthly relationships. The more we know, love and trust someone, the more faith we have in them and the more we remain faithful in that relationship. First Corinthians 14:1 tells us not only to be faithful in love but to pursue love. What does that look like? It looks like pursuing people – not running from them nor hiding from them. Just do it! Pursue love with patience and grace.

Did you know that the apostle Paul actually left a ministry trip to pursue love – to find his friend, Titus? We see that in 2 Corinthians 2:12-13 (NKJV), "Furthermore, when I came to Troas to preach Christ's gospel, and a door was opened to me by the Lord, I had no rest in my spirit, because I did not find Titus my brother; but taking my leave of them, I departed for Macedonia."

DON'T WITHDRAW LOVE

Jesus never stopped loving His disciples ... His friends. John 13:1 says, "He loved them to the end." They were not perfect and, of course, neither are we. Sometimes the disciples disappointed Jesus, but His love was unconditional. May we never forget that He loves us to the end, too, and will never leave nor forsake us (Hebrews 13:5). Our goal should be the same, even though maintaining relationships may not always be easy. There can be disappointments, misunderstandings and conflict along the way, but remember, our God is faithful and is looking for faithfulness. He loves to restore love!

A SERVANT HEART

Jesus came to serve – and His ultimate act of service was giving His life so that we may be restored to God (see John 15:13; Philippians 2:5-11). There will be times when restoration will require such a servant heart. Ask yourself: Are there things I need to lay down so I can serve others with excellence? Are the things I'm doing good or God?

As faithful friends, hopefully we can discern when others need help and then adjust our busy schedules to serve more. Don't forget that Jesus, our main mentor, had a ministry of interruptions. Ecclesiastes 4:10 (NKJV) teaches us to be there for our friends. "For if they fall, one will lift up his companion. But woe to him who is alone when he falls, for he has no one to help him up."

JUST START

"If you love Me, keep My commandments" – John 14:15 (13:34; 15:9; 15:10; 15:12; 15:16). Love is something we are commanded to do. When we're obedient to that command we find that the more we love, *the more we want to love.* We reach a point where we no longer love out of obedience; we love because we long to. God is love – and we are able to love Him, then others, because He first loved us.

73

Oftentimes people speak about love, but a person who knows how to be a faithful friend truly understands love – God's love. Let's be one of those people.

How's your love barometer compared to 1 Corinthians 13?

Love is patient, love is kind and is not jealous; love does not brag and is not arrogant, does not act unbecomingly; it does not seek its own, is not provoked, does not take into account a wrong suffered, does not rejoice in unrighteousness, but rejoices with the truth; bears all things, believes all things, hopes all things, endures all things. Love never fails.
– 1 Corinthians 13:4-8

May I suggest that you quiet your soul and listen for the voice of your Shepherd (John 10:27) as He speaks to your heart or brings people (or situations) to your remembrance (John 14:27) who are lacking in love – your love. Pray about your role in restoring these relationships and take the first step.

RESTORATION OF LOVE

Have you ever been around someone with a broken heart who then says, "I will never love again! I'd rather die." Well, here's the deal. If we don't love, we're already dead, because God is love. We're created to receive love and to give love.

The loss or inability to love will actually be a warning sign before Christ's second coming: "Because lawlessness is increased, most people's love will grow cold." (Matthew 24:12)

Be cautious and don't let YOUR love grow cold. The enemy wants to drag issues of life on for years and years. Don't allow that. Don't let the past ruin your future. March forward.

Love is God's nature, period. In Romans 8:35, the Word of God asks what will separate us from the love of Christ, and then we find the answer in verses 37-39:

> In all these things we overwhelmingly conquer through Him who loved us. For I am convinced that neither death, nor life, nor angels, nor principalities, nor things present, nor things to come, nor powers, nor height, nor depth, nor any other created thing, will be able to separate us from the love of God, which is in Christ Jesus our Lord.

There you have it! **Nothing** can separate us from God's love – a love so great that He sent His only Son to die for us.

When we fully know that God loves us and that nothing can separate us from that love, then even during dark times, times of brokenness, we can believe that His love can restore our faith in love. We always have a starting block to go back to as we run the race of life – it's called love. In fact, each start-over can help us grow in love and learn to better love with agape love. Agape love is God's love. It's Christian love and is always concerned for the welfare of one another.

RESTORING THE FAMILY BRIDGE

> "He will also go before Him in the spirit and power of Elijah, 'to turn the hearts of the fathers to the children and the disobedient to the wisdom of the just, to make ready a people prepared for the Lord.'" – Luke 1:17 (NKJV)

We cannot turn the heart of another. But, we are responsible for our own heart. Following are some keys for family connections (bridges).

- TALK.

- Be kind.

- Don't be critical.

- Do not provoke.

- Be humble.

- Listen with intent to hear.

- Say "I'm sorry."

- Choose your words wisely. (Death and life are in the power of the tongue. – Proverbs 18:22)

- Parents, make a conscious choice to turn your heart to your children. Do not turn away.

- Children, make a conscious choice to turn your heart to your parents. Do not turn away.

- Do not withdraw love.

- Forgive.

- Let go of offense; it will not let go of you. We choose what we take on.

- Choose to love.

- Take the axe to the root of bitterness.

- Trust God, the Restorer.

ACTION STEPS – RESTORING BURNED BRIDGES

Pray – Trust Holy Spirit when He's nudging you to restore a burned bridge, and begin praying for grace and wisdom on how to cooperate with Him. He leads you into triumph (2 Corinthians 2:14).

Pursue – Start with a phone call, an email, some form of polite communication to break the ice. Even a friendly "hello" is a start and can begin rebuilding the bridge between people – brick by brick.

Be honest – Don't beat around the bush and play games. Let the other party know that you respect them and would like to talk. Let them know that you really want to hear their heart in the matter.

Love – We restore burned bridges because we love, and the Word says love never fails. Focus on the one you have an agape love for, not on the hurts or wounds, whether yours or theirs. What you focus on, you will empower. Focusing on others and praying for them prepares them to become receptive to your invitation to restore.

Cross the restored bridge – Forget the former things and move forward. Unresolved issues may need to be discussed but try to keep this step brief, if possible, and move on. Don't get trapped in the past by the enemy.

Invite – Try to involve the other party in bridging the gap. What do they need to help them feel safe? How do they feel about all of this? How do they want to proceed?

Trust God – We can initiate rebuilding, but we can't control the final results. Stay low and trust God.

Say you're sorry – Be ready and willing to apologize for your role in the burned bridge. Take responsibility. This will not fix everything, but it's a great place to begin. Ask for forgiveness and give it.

Bury the hatchet – Be kind and gentle, and no matter how much you are tempted to repeat old scenarios – don't do it! Be sensitive to what you think might be triggers for the other person. Don't go there.

Respond, don't react – When communicating, listen to the speaker's heart. Don't react defensively or out of anger or woundedness. Take a deep breath and let Holy Spirit season your speech with grace before you respond. If you're developing a clever or ungodly answer while someone is talking, you aren't really listening.

Believe the best and pray the rest – There's no guarantee that things will work out right away. Broken things take time to heal, like a broken bone. Keep your eyes on Jesus, as He is the Redeemer. The Hebrew word for redeemer is *goel*. It means "one charged with the duty of restoring the rights of another and avenging his wrongs."

CHAPTER NINE

Choosing Honor

NON-NEGOTIABLE

An often overlooked key to restoration is honor. The Bible is very clear about honor. Honoring is huge to God and can change our lives. If things are not going well with a boss, spouse or friend, stop and ask yourself if you are honoring them. The choice to give honor where it is due can bring about advancement, while dishonor can have the opposite effect. If you absolutely cannot seem to honor someone in authority, then honor the position that they are in (see Romans 13:1-7). Or, if you are really struggling to honor someone who caused a horrible offense, then at least honor by not dishonoring. Honor is a Kingdom principle that is non-negotiable. It changes relationships and you will reap what you sow.

WHO ARE WE TO HONOR?

PARENTS – "Honor your father and your mother, that your days may be prolonged in the land which the Lord your God gives you" (Exodus 20:12).

THOSE IN AUTHORITY – Romans 13:1-7 explains that God, in His sovereignty, has placed people in positions of leadership. In this context, verse 7 says that you should give to everyone what you owe them: If you owe taxes, pay taxes; if revenue, then revenue; if respect, then respect; if honor, then honor.

CHURCH LEADERS – The elders who direct the affairs of the church well are worthy of double honor, especially those whose work is preaching and teaching (1 Timothy 5:17).

EACH OTHER – "Be devoted to one another in brotherly love; give preference to one another in honor" (Romans 12:10). Why? Because we see the reflection of Christ in them. They were created in Christ's image and reveal God's nature, His attributes, and His power.

David is a great example of someone who learned to honor even in an extremely tough situation. He took measures to not be in harm's way, yet until the very end he treated with honor the one who had betrayed his trust, loyalty and care (see 1 Samuel 24). If you are in a difficult situation, please remember that dishonor can be telling everyone who will listen what a terrible person/situation you are dealing with. But seeking godly counsel to help you make wise – and often tough – decisions is showing honor.

Well, there you have it. If you glance back at our list, you will see that we are to honor *everyone*. Let's be co-laborers with Christ as He restores honor to His people.

ABOVE ALL – HONOR GOD

It's crucial to give and receive honor in order for restoration to take place. It's also crucial to draw on God's amazing grace and remember that He honored His creation so much that even from the very beginning He had a plan of redemption – a plan to convert turmoil on the earth to restoration of all things.

When we glorify God, we bring Him honor. When we honor Him, we are demonstrating the high regard we have for Him. We're reflecting His glory back to Him in the church, family or marketplace as praise, worship, teaching, leading, serving and so on.

Definitions

Old Testament

In the Old Testament, honor is defined as *dóksa* (from *dokeō*, DOXA) – which is glory. Honor also corresponds to the Old Testament word *kabod* ("to be heavy or weighty"). Both terms convey God's infinite worth (substance).

New Testament

In the New Testament, DOXA is defined as praise, honor, glorify, majesty – meaning that something or someone has inherent, intrinsic worth.

To honor God, we give Him regard, reverence, awe, praise, submission, adoration, awe, and obedience due to Him. We worship God in all our lives with attitudes and actions. The substance of what it means to honor God is revealed to us in what Jesus called the first and greatest commandment:

> You shall love the Lord your God with all your heart, and with all your soul, and with all your mind. This is the great and first commandment.   – Matthew 22:37–38

ASCRIBING HONOR

It's sad to say, but if we look around, we can see vast amounts of dishonor on the earth. This is not the will of God. The source of all honor is God, based on His position as the Creator. God the Father lavished honor on His Son, Jesus Christ (John 5:23). He lavished honor on humanity by creating man a little lower than the angels (Psalm 8:5-6). God also created spheres of authority within human government, the church, and the home.

Since God is our Teacher, who sends us to teach the world, if we dishonor Him it only makes sense that dishonor is going to flow down from us, the church, to the world. Therefore, it's our responsibility to cultivate honor.

Since God has no faults, we honor Him and allow that honor to flow into our hearts and spheres of influence. In Isaiah 29:13 (NIV), The Lord says: "These people come near to Me with their mouth and honor Me with their lips, but their hearts are far from Me." Let's not be those people. Honor is a matter of the heart – a choice. We learn to honor because we want to, not because we have to.

Jesus came to earth to reveal God and His attributes. God is clearly revealed in Jesus and in the Bible. Anything other than what we see in the Bible leads to darkness, not to restoration.

Take note of what Romans 1:21 (NLT) says:

Yes, they knew God, but they wouldn't worship him as God or even give him thanks. And they began to think up foolish ideas of what God was like. As a result, their minds became dark and confused.

To love someone, to have a strong, healthy relationship with them, we need to know them, right? We need to, and we want to. We want to know their attributes, their characteristics. We want to know all about their nature and know their qualities.

Let's take a look at some attributes of God, so we can see

where we might fall short and need honor restored. If we truly honor God, then we will honor the people He created.

ATTRIBUTES OF GOD

Holiness: In the highest sense, holiness pertains to God. Holiness also belongs to Christians, set apart to be conformed. Holiness sets God apart from every created being on earth and in heaven. It radiates glory and total righteousness.

Infinitude: God is endless; He knows no boundaries and is immeasurable. Infinitude affects every other attribute.

Omniscience: God knows everything! It is impossible to hide anything from God.

Sovereignty: God rules HIS creation. ALL of it. Yes, He's given man free will and that free will includes taking responsibility for our choices. So we, as the body of Christ, CHOOSE to honor the attributes of God.

Trinity: Honor is given to the Father, Son, and Holy Spirit. Let's be sure that we know each person of the Trinity. "Everyone will honor the Son, just as they honor the Father. Anyone who does not honor the Son is certainly not honoring the Father who sent him" (John 5:23 NLT).

Wisdom: Wisdom is a gift from God to those who ask for it. "Wisdom" in Proverbs 1:20; 8:1; 9:1-5 is not regarded as just an attribute but as a divine person, "Christ the power of God and the wisdom of God" (1 Corinthians 1:24). God does not make any mistakes. Do we truly HONOR wisdom?

Faithfulness: Everything that God has promised will come to pass. The Bible is Truth. God is Truth. Jesus is Truth. With faith, all things are possible!!

What if God didn't honor His own attributes? Then our sins wouldn't be forgiven. We wouldn't live eternally.

LIVING EPISTLES

WE lead the way! That's why God says GO and TEACH.

In walking this out, let's remember that Christ went from the lowest place of humility to the highest place of honor, and He took us with Him. He elevated us to sons and daughters of the Most High God, and we may be the only Jesus that many people see.

Let's BE honor and show the world that honor brings life. Christ honored you on the cross. He gave His life for you, and that honor gives abundant life. God shows us in the fourth commandment that when we honor, we have long life. However, if we pridefully dishonor, there are consequences. We see what happens in Proverbs 18:12 which says, "Before his downfall [destruction] a man's heart is proud, but humility comes before honor."

When we honor God, we become vessels of honor. We carry His truth and His love and serve as His ambassadors.

God will be honored as the Creator of everything in heaven and earth, and in due time every knee will bow. Psalm 46:10 (NLT) says it like this, "Be still, and know that I am God! I will be honored by every nation. I will be honored throughout the world."

Revelation 7:12 shows us how to live on earth, as it is in heaven. It says, "Amen, blessing and glory and wisdom and thanksgiving and honor and power and might, be to our God forever and ever. Amen."

I pray that honor is restored to God and man, so you can live in such a way that those who know you but don't know God will come to know God because they know you.

WAYS TO HONOR GOD

Make a list of ways you can honor God – not because you have to but because you want to. What are your strong areas of honor? What areas need to be strengthened?

Example:

Faithfulness in tithing – "Honor the Lord from your wealth and from the first of all your produce; So your barns will be filled with plenty and your vats will overflow with new wine" (Proverbs 3:9-10). Let's give God what's right, not what's left.

CHAPTER TEN

What Does God Restore?

BLESSED TO BE A BLESSING

Since we serve a God of restoration, we might ask the question: "What can God restore?" The answer is that God can restore *everything* that has been lost; nothing is impossible with Him (Luke 1:37). Whatever has been lost in your life, whatever has been stolen, and whatever has been taken from you, God is able to restore it. Not only that, but whatever you have willingly given up for God can be restored, too.

Let's look at Abraham who willingly climbed Mount Moriah with his son Isaac, preparing to sacrifice him in obedience to God's command. As Abraham raised the knife above his son's head, God called out, "Stop! Now I know that you love Me." Because Abraham was willing to give up his promised son, God gave him many sons in return, making him the "father of many nations." Jesus also promises restoration in Matthew 19:29, which says, "Everyone who has left houses or brothers or sisters or father or mother or wife or children or lands, for My name's sake, shall receive a hundredfold, and inherit eternal life." In other words, what we give up, God gives back.

What have you sacrificed, friend? Have you given up money or time? What has been taken from you – your health, your joy, your marriage, or your business? I'm here to shout from the rooftops that God is about to restore what the enemy has taken from you. He clearly showed me that there will be a harvest before the Great Harvest. We are about to see the greatest harvest of souls known to mankind, and it's important to be blessed to be a blessing to thousands.

SPECIFICS

Strength

How wonderful it is to cling to God's promises and know that He restores strength, energy, passion, and motivation, even in old age. The women said to Naomi toward the end of her life, after she had lost her husband and her sons: "And may [God] be to you a restorer of life and a nourisher of your old age" (Ruth 4:15 NKJV).

Flesh

God can restore your flesh: " 'Now put it back into your cloak,' he said. So Moses put his hand back into his cloak, and when he took it out, it was restored, like the rest of his flesh" (Exodus 4:7 NIV).

God used this miracle to confirm His power to Moses and the Israelites. That's exactly what God wants to do today. We are going to see more and more miracles, and more of God's power as He is glorified on the earth!

I have seen this and many other restoration miracles firsthand. I have a friend whose needle marks from a past life of drug use completely disappeared, and new, beautiful skin appeared.

Here's another Scripture to build your faith. "His flesh will be fresher than a child's; he will return to the days of his youth" (Job 33:25 KJV). Now, that's amazing, because Job's skin was covered with boils and he was reduced to skin and bone. But God promised that his health would be restored, and his skin would be healthy and smooth. And it was healed, along with multiple restorations and great increase in his life.

One more verse, just in case you're having a difficult time believing the extraordinary promises of God.

> "Then he [Naaman] went down, and dipped himself seven times in the Jordan, according to the saying of the man of God: and his flesh came again like the flesh of a little child, and he was clean" (2 Kings 5:14 AKJV).

Naaman was captain of the host of the king of Syria. He was a great man and highly esteemed for his military character and success. He was also wealthy and a mighty man of valor. But, unfortunately, he was a leper. Leprosy would have excluded him from society and is fatal. God sent a messenger who told Naaman to dip in the river seven times and his flesh would be healed.

Perhaps the Lord will give you specific instructions for restoration. He is the God of miracles yesterday, today and forever.

If you have tattoos you wish you didn't have, scars from cutting, needle marks, burns or perhaps a skin disease, today is a great day for the Lord to restore!

Property

If you have lost property, then know that God is able to restore that as well. Take a look at 2 Samuel 9:7 (NKJV): "So David said to him, 'Do not fear, for I will surely show you kindness for Jonathan your father's sake, and will restore to you all the land of Saul your grandfather; and you shall eat bread at my table continually.'"

And another: "I will also show you compassion, so that he will have compassion on you and restore you to your own soil [land]" (Jeremiah 42:12 NASB).

I would encourage you to read 2 Kings 8:1-6, as your faith is stirred. In the story of the Shunammite woman we see her son's life restored and then she appeals to the king for restoration of her house and her land. The king restores ALL that is hers – a powerful lesson on how we can appeal to the true Kings of Kings for restoration of houses, land and all!

Positions

Did you ever wish that you could start over again? Do you want to turn back the hands of time and recover positions that were stolen by the enemy? Well, I have good news for you. Positions can be recovered.

Take a look at Genesis 40:21 (NKJV). "Then he **restored** the chief butler to his butlership again, and he placed the cup in Pharaoh's hand." Alleluia! That's our God right there. He is the God of restoration and He has no favorites; if He did it for the butler, He will do it for you!

In fact, according to Joel 2:25-26 (NKJV), the Lord can even restore time. "I will restore [replace] to you the years that the swarming locust has eaten ... You shall eat in plenty and be satisfied, and praise the name of the Lord your God, who has dealt wondrously with you; and My people shall never be put to shame."

God wants to restore what you have lost. He has new beginnings for you. He has new opportunities, hopes and dreams for you.

Lives

There are many reasons why lives may need restoration. Perhaps persecution took its toll, maybe a life was shattered by horrific tragedy, or sometimes people experience extremely long seasons of preparation – like Moses – and then they are restored to their divine purpose. And, of course there are lives that need restoration following a painful fall into sin.

It's always very sad to see someone fall into sin. A fall can take you from paradise to ashamed nakedness in a moment. Sometimes a trespass can devastate an entire church or destroy a long-term covenant. But it's wonderful to know that our God of mercy, compassion, and love can restore those who fall! He says in Galatians 6:1 (NKJV), "Brethren, if a man is overtaken in any trespass, you who are spiritual restore such a one in a spirit of gentleness, considering yourself lest you also be tempted." (We could substitute for the word "trespass" and say, "If a man is overtaken by persecution or tragedy, restore such a one").

If you think about it, God began restoring lives "in the beginning." We see the fall of man when Adam and Eve sinned against God, but even then He already had a plan in place to send a Redeemer/Restorer to the world. So fear not! No matter where we fit into the equation of a fall, let's remember that mercy triumphs over judgment – judgment doesn't triumph over mercy.

God not only restores lives, but He then uses those lives to bring restoration to others. To say it another way, Paul writes, "[He] comforts us in all our tribulation, that we may be able to comfort those who are in any trouble, with the comfort with which we ourselves are comforted by God" (2 Corinthians 1:4 NKJV).

No matter how much devastation has crept into a life, there will always be more grace. Maybe you think you're a great sinner, but listen, Jesus is a great Savior. The Lord is the master at fixing disasters.

Lives Restored

Joseph

God gave him a dream.

He boasted of his dream.

He was thrown into the pit.

He was put into the prison.

He was raised to the palace.

Moses

He was groomed to be a leader – in line to be the pharaoh.

God gave him a vision to be a deliverer of his people.

He became a shepherd for 40 years.

He became the Great Deliverer.

Jesus

He was born to be King of kings.

He had a very lowly birth.

He was oppressed and afflicted.

He was accused and sentenced to be crucified.

He died, was buried, and was RESURRECTED to be King of kings forever.

Health

If our health has been stolen, we know that God is the one who restores it. He said through Jeremiah, " 'For I will restore health to you and heal you of your wounds,' says the Lord" (Jeremiah 30:17 NKJV). We are co-laborers with Christ and must cooperate with Holy Spirit, our Helper, to enhance the restoration process. And, when God gives us health and wholeness, it is our responsibility to maintain it.

I could list well over 100 Scriptures on healing here, but I'll hold back – smile. However, you might want to take time to do a word search on healing – you will see that God is serious about restoring health!

"He pardons all your iniquities, He heals all your diseases" (Psalm 103:3).

"He heals the brokenhearted and binds up their wounds (Psalm 147:3).

"I, the Lord, am your healer" (Exodus 15:26).

The Lord will sustain him upon his sickbed;
In his illness, You restore him to health" (Psalm 41:3).

Words of Protection

- When we take God out of medicine, it's like taking prayer out of schools.

- Try not to give infirmity substance. Proverbs 18:21 warns us that, "Death and life are in the power of the tongue."

  So, yes, we need to gather facts, but then seek Truth, and proclaim God's promises to heal.

A word about medicines. We are certainly thankful for the great advances in modern-day medicine and their benefits. However, they can be overused and abused, causing serious side effects.

Consider the following:

- Most drugs merely produce the opposite effect of the symptoms. That does not define healing.

- At least sixty to seventy percent of television advertisements are about diseases and medications.

- Death caused by over-the-counter and prescription medication is ten times greater than that caused by illegal drugs.

- Take a preventative approach. Although you may need to take medicines, use them as a last resort ... not the solution to everything. Practice a healthy lifestyle – physically, emotionally, and spiritually. It is strongly implied in 3 John 2 that our soul – that is, our will, emotions, decisions, reasoning, choices, thoughts – is the source of many (or all?) health issues. Take care of your soul! Don't hesitate to seek sound counsel, healing prayer, and freedom ministry when needed, so that you can prosper. "Beloved, I pray that you may prosper in all things and be in health, just as your soul prospers" (3 John 2 NKJV).

- Jesus is the Healer! "Surely He has borne our griefs and carried our sorrows. Yet we esteemed Him stricken, smitten by God, and afflicted. But He was wounded for our transgressions, He was bruised for our iniquities; the chastisement for our peace was upon Him, and by *His stripes we are healed*" (Isaiah 53:4-5 NKJV).

PRAYER FOR HEALING

Father God, I come to Your throne boldly and thank You for Your amazing grace. I thank You for Your Living Word, and I embrace Your promises to heal me. I believe Your Word. I declare it with my mouth – I am healed of all disease and sickness!

Thank You for sending Your Son to bear all sickness and disease, and for carrying my sorrows. I receive healing right now. I declare, "Jesus, You are MY Healer." I praise You for giving me all that I need for restoration so I can live in wholeness.

Thank You for abundant life. I rejoice in knowing that You show no favoritism. What You do for another, You do for me. I come asking, believing, and thanking You, by faith.

I declare in the name of Jesus that the devil has no authority over me, because I have been redeemed of the curse, restored, and I am hidden in God. You said in Matthew 18:18 that we can bind the devil from operating against us, so I do that right now in Your powerful name. And I loose the glory of God, all that You have and all that You are, into my entire being. I AM HEALED. I AM RESTORED.

MORE SPECIFICS

Finances

Remember that earlier we looked at Acts 3:20–21, which showed us that the church is in the process of "times of restoration." Well, that certainly includes restoration of finances. What a great time to be alive – only believe.

Here are a couple of Scriptures to help you believe and receive:

"Then Joseph gave a command to fill their sacks with grain, *to restore* every man's money to his sack, and to give them provisions for the journey."   – Genesis 42:25 (NKJV)

"Give away your life; you'll find life given back, but not merely given back – given back with bonus and blessing. Giving, not getting, is the way. Generosity begets generosity."   – Luke 6:38 (MSG)

Begin - or continue – to sow and reap! Don't hold back, friend. Be aware of a withholding spirit that lies and is the exact opposite of generosity. If you sow sparingly, you will reap sparingly. Jesus was a giver – He gave His life. Let's learn from Him and see amazing restoration.

"Give generously and generous gifts will be given back to you, shaken down to make room for more. Abundant gifts will pour out upon you with such an overflowing measure that it will run over the top! Your measurement of generosity becomes the measurement of your return." – Luke 6:38 (TPT)

Let's remember here that Jesus didn't come to restore a poverty demon. He came to cast it out. Poverty is horrible; it kills people by starving them to death. Abundance that comes from the Lord feeds the world.

Souls and Prosperity

God promises to restore the damages that have taken place in our soul so that we can prosper once again:

"He restores my soul; He leads me in the paths of righteousness for His name's sake."   – Psalm 23:3 (NKJV)

"Beloved, I pray that you may prosper in all things and be in health, just as your soul prospers."   – 3 John 2 (NKJV)

"What will it profit a man if he gains the whole world and forfeits his soul? Or what shall a man give in return for his soul?"   – Matthew 16:26 (ESV)

Perhaps you're in a place in life where you could say, "I lost me. I feel empty and I need God to restore my soul." Well, that's okay because it's a great day for restoration.

The soul is a person's inner person, their identity and inner self. It includes their personality, mind and heart, will and emotions. Your soul cannot be isolated from the rest of you. Therefore, if your soul prospers, all things prosper.

In the beginning, according to Genesis 2:7, "The Lord God formed the man of dust from the ground and breathed into his nostrils the breath of life, and the man became a living soul" (KJV).

Proverbs 4:23 says it's out of the heart [soul] that all life flows. Wow! Your whole life has to do with the condition of your soul. Your heart and soul are the essence of who you are. That's why the Bible says to guard your heart *above all else.* Think of it this way. If your physical heart dies, you're a goner. It's the same with your spiritual heart – if it dies, you're a goner. The heart is under constant attack by the accuser of the brethren because he comes to destroy (John 10:10). We must guard against disappointment, stress, discouragement, and stress. Hey, stress can kill you!

If we're going to ask God to restore our soul, it's important to know the state of our soul. How do you know if your soul is hurt, not prospering? Let's take a look at a few red flags.

• Is it difficult for you to fall asleep? Do you only sleep for short periods of time?

- Are you excited to live an abundant life, or does life seem dull and overwhelming?

- Do you find yourself short tempered with people? Do your emotional buttons go off easily and, instantly, you react to people rather than responding to them?

- Do you get angry frequently, even over small issues?

- Do you struggle with alcohol or drug abuse? How about overeating or binge eating?

- Would you rather be alone most of the time than be around people? Do you feel alone?

- Are you confused and upset? Does there seem to be inner turmoil that you just can't fix?

- Are you experiencing prolonged, unhealthy grief? Are you full of sorrow and sadness?

- Does it seem like nothing is going right? Does everything seem like a failure, even you?

These red flags *do not* mean you are bad, they mean you are hurt. They mean you need help. Everyone has some damage to their soul, but just because people have broken hearts, broken families or broken marriages doesn't mean they have to remain broken the rest of their lives. As with most problems, admitting we need help is the first step to recovery/restoration. The soul is meant for abundant life, and when God restores your soul, you will feel alive again and your joy will return.

"He restores my soul" in Psalm 23 is a promise, and it means "to refresh." The thing is, we cannot restore ourselves. God is the one who will put us back together again and give us wholeness. Spend time with Him and rest. We can't be refreshed if we've become adrenaline junkies. Find prayer partners to help you through this; don't suffer in silence. Take a sabbatical if necessary. Take long walks, read and listen to music. And finally, rejoice as the darkness lifts off your soul, you are restored and enjoying abundant life.

Time

God can supernaturally restore time. One of our key Scriptures on restoration highlights this.

> "So I will restore to you the years that the swarming locust has eaten, the crawling locust, the consuming locust, and the chewing locust."   – Joel 2:25 (NKJV)

"How can God restore time?" we ask; that seems impossible. Well, first of all, nothing is impossible for God, and secondly, this is not an intellectual matter, it's a supernatural one. So, we don't lean on our own understanding, we lean on God. He can and does take years that were stolen or wasted and accelerates things in your life so you can catch up, so to speak.

Let's take a look at a contemporary scenario so you grasp this and receive restoration of time. Mr. Somebody had a business partner who was attacked by the locust of greediness. Over a period of five years this partner swindled Mr. Somebody out of $10,000 dollars. Well, God's promise to restore years is just as valid today as it was in the Old Testament. He restored the $10,000 dollars to Mr. Somebody and multiplied it seven times. So now, Mr. Somebody had $70,000 dollars, was extremely fruitful, and accomplished more in one year than he could have in seven years. Years restored. Boom!

And, take a look at Mrs. Somebody, who suffered from an addiction to drugs. This devouring locust stole many years of her life. But when she found out that *where the spirit of the Lord is, there is freedom*, she was set free from addiction and restored. Consequently, she wanted to go back to school and fulfill her dreams, the dreams of God. When Mrs. Somebody enrolled in college she had the supernatural favor of God surrounding her. With transfer credits and excellent performance and test results, her degree only took her two and a half years rather than four. There you have it! She gained years right there.

Joel 2:27 says, "You will know that I am in the midst of Israel [and you], and that I am the Lord your God." Here we see the greatest restoration of all. When the locusts devour years, it often brings people to their knees, and that is a wonderful place to meet God on a personal, intimate level. With that relationship secured, He becomes Lord of our lives and not only are years restored, but all of eternity. That's quite an increase!

Joy – And last, but certainly not least, if we become discouraged, we must remember that God is the One who restores our joy. When we lose our joy, it's usually not a sudden event. No, the enemy is sly, and slowly over time he steals your joy. It's important to admit we lost it and ask God for restoration: "Restore to me the joy of Your salvation, and uphold me by Your generous Spirit" (Psalm 51:12). God is always ready to fight for you! He knows that the joy of the Lord is our strength – if we lose our joy, we lose our strength.

It's always important to understand what we're asking for. So let's be clear on the fact that happiness and joy are very different. Happiness is a feeling. When things in your life are going very well, you feel happy, based on your circumstances at the time.

However, joy is gladness, well-being and delight. It can be totally independent of circumstances. Joy is a Hebrew word that means *exceeding* joy or glee. Joy is from the Lord, it flows from heaven and fills us because we are certain that no matter what happens, God can use it for good even though it looks bad at the moment.

Here is Psalm 30:11: "You have turned for me my mourning into dancing." How great is that?

It's God who restores joy; that's why it's important to spend time in His Presence and learn to take His Presence with you all the time. Psalm 16:11 reads, "You [God] will make known to me the path of life; *In Your presence is fullness of joy.*"

Please allow me to expand on my testimony of joy that I mentioned in chapter one. I lost my joy about twenty-five years ago. I remember my oldest son saying, "Ma, please stop crying. You've been crying for a year." Boy, did I need to hear that. Sometimes we don't honestly see what we're doing until someone points it out to us for our own good. I stopped crying (mostly), but how could I get my joy back?

I asked God and, guess what, HE did it. One day following the message at church we were invited to come to the altar if we needed prayer; man, did I need prayer! I think I was the first one up there. While a precious couple was praying for me I was slain in the Spirit by the power and presence of God. This was a first for me. I remember people continuing to pray for me, and I thought to myself, "How did I get from the front of the church to the back?" That's when I heard God speak to my heart. He spoke only two words, "Joy unspeakable." I realized later that my body hadn't actually moved from the front of the church to the back, but spiritually speaking I had been flowing in the River of Restoration. During those few moments of time I was changed forever. To this very day, I am almost always joyful.

Joy fills our hearts when we remember all of the good things God has done for us and look forward to great things to come. Joy is restored when we trust and know that better days are just around the bend!

"Oh, the joys of those who trust the Lord…"

– Psalm 40:4 NLT

WHAT DO YOU NEED RESTORED?

Try making a list and find a prayer partner, or prayer team, if necessary. Don't hesitate to do this, because agreeing with someone in prayer is very powerful. Take a look at Matthew 18:19 (NKJV): "If two of you agree on earth concerning anything that they ask, it will be done for them by My Father in heaven." And how about Mark 11:24 (NKJV)? "Therefore, I say to you, whatever things you ask when you pray, believe that you receive them, and you will have them." What a powerful promise.

Pray these Scriptures out loud and insert the areas of your life that need restoration. Suppose you need joy restored; you could pray, "We agree on earth for restoration of my joy and, in asking, we know that it will be done by my Father in heaven." Find other relevant Scriptures in the Bible – read them and write them. That's a great way to learn – Read it, Write it, Say it! As you take these action steps, restoration will become part of your identity in Christ.

CHAPTER ELEVEN

The Storms of Life

Question: What happens before restoration?

Answer: Usually something is damaged or demolished first or it wouldn't need restoring.

Ecclesiastes 3:3 tells us that to everything there is a season, including, "A time to tear down and a time to build up." It's very important to recognize what time and season we are in so we don't miss the restoration opportunity and process.

NAVIGATING STORMS

Are there storms in your life? There certainly are plenty in the world. It's important to be prepared for storms even during restoration or, perhaps I should say, especially during restoration. Restoration is wonderful, but it often shakes up the status quo. Be prepared, and don't be surprised if you start to encounter hurricane behavior around you for a while as you grow by leaps and bounds. Change is good, but not always comfortable.

Storms can cause an excessive amount of damage if we don't know how to manage them. The Lord clearly teaches us how to remain calm during storms and use them to strengthen our faith, trusting as we draw near to the great I AM. It's when we trust God during what seems like demolition that He can turn things around for our good. When we draw close to the Lord, He uses the mighty winds in our lives to help us get where we're going ... "immediately."

Storms can become hands-on training times when God molds us to become more like His Son, for that's the eternal goal.

> We know that God causes everything to work together for the good of those who love God and are called according to his purpose for them. For God knew his people in advance, and he chose them to become like his Son, so that his Son would be the firstborn among many brothers and sisters.
>
> – Romans 8:28–29 (NLT)

WALK ON WATER

The disciples sure knew about storms. The Bible recalls a time when they were in trouble far away from land:

> ...for a strong wind had risen, and they were fighting heavy waves. About three o'clock in the morning Jesus came toward them, walking on the water. When the disciples saw him walking on the water, they were terrified. In their fear, they cried out, "It's a ghost!" But Jesus spoke to them at once. *"Don't be afraid,"* he said. "Take courage. I am here!" Then Peter called to him, "Lord, if it's really you, tell me to come to you, walking on the water." "Yes, come," Jesus said. So Peter went over the side of the boat and walked on the water toward Jesus. But when he saw the strong wind and the waves, he was terrified and began to sink. "Save me, Lord!" he shouted. Jesus immediately reached out and grabbed him. *"You have so little faith,"* Jesus said. "Why did you doubt me?"

When they climbed back into the boat, the wind stopped. Then the disciples worshiped him. "You really are the Son of God!" they exclaimed.   – Matthew 14:22-33 (NLT)

When we're braving the gale-force winds of life, it's important to stay focused on the Lord and remember that those winds and waves can accelerate our destiny if we manage them well. Isn't it amazing that Peter could miraculously walk on water as long as he was focused on Jesus, but he began to sink when he focused on the invasion? Often, it's when we quiet our emotions and get real still that we can hear our Father saying, "I am here. I will always be right here beside you." And then we know in our spirit that God is not testing our ability to walk on water, but He may be testing our faith.

Question: When did Peter walk on water, experiencing a miracle?

Answer: During the storm. Selah.

In another lesson, we see Elijah was running for his life and desperate to hear from God. Then he was told,

"Go, stand on the mountain at attention before God. God will pass by." A hurricane wind ripped through the mountains and shattered the rocks before God, but God wasn't to be found in the wind; after the wind an earthquake, but God wasn't in the earthquake; and after the earthquake fire, but God wasn't in the fire; and after the fire a gentle and quiet whisper.   – 1 Kings 19:11-12 (MSG)

Question: When did Elijah hear God's voice?

Answer: After the storm. Selah.

God speaks in many different ways and at different times. He's a personal God and knows you even better than you know yourself. He knows what you will respond to, what will get your attention, and how to reach you with His love. As we grow spiritually and emotionally we learn to trust God in the storms. We learn to stand on the Word just like Peter did when Jesus said, "Come." Peter was able to stand on His Word in faith, and walk the stormy waters, trusting God in what seemed like an impossible situation. When we are facing a storm, let's get our Bibles out and find the Word of the Lord that He wants us to stand on. Memorize it, declare it, live it. We shall not be moved!

STRATEGIES FOR NAVIGATING STORMS

Trust

Let's take a look at how our trust in God, or in any relationship, is built so we have safety nets [people] in place when storms hit. There's safety in numbers.

One great way is by exchanging truth back and forth; that builds trust.

Another way is to role-model trust. In the Scriptures, Jesus wasn't just asking Peter to walk on water, He was asking Peter to be like Him – to imitate the things that He did.

A common bond can help build trust. When we befriend someone who has had experiences similar to ours, it's usually easy to learn to trust them.

Time helps build trust, because it needs to be earned.

Receive Jesus

When we read John 6:16-21 we find another way to maneuver through the storms of life.

When evening came, His disciples went down to the sea, and after getting into a boat, they started to cross the sea to Capernaum. It had already become dark, and Jesus had not yet come to them. The sea began to be stirred up because a strong wind was blowing. Then, when they had rowed about three or four miles, they saw Jesus walking on the sea and drawing near to the boat; and they were frightened. But He said to them, "It is I; do not be afraid." So they were willing to receive Him into the boat, and immediately the boat was at the land to which they were going.

Question: What's the fastest way to get through a storm and get to where you want to go?

Answer: Invite Jesus into the equation. Receive Him into your heart.

Rest in Him

Mark 4:38-39 is another great example of how Jesus trusted His Father and knew the authority that He carried. Right in the middle of a huge storm at sea, Jesus was inside the boat, sleeping. His followers went and woke Him and said, "Teacher, don't you care about us? We are going to drown!" Jesus stood up and commanded the wind and the water. He said, "Quiet! Be still!" Then the wind stopped, and the lake became calm.

When we are restored to wholeness we learn to rest, like Jesus did, even in the midst of trials and tribulations. We become acutely aware that God is in control, we are not. As believers, we also learn that the authority of Christ dwells in us. We can speak to the storms rather than becoming passive and missing the restoration at hand. Prayer changes things.

Know He Is with You

You might find that as you're restored – made whole – the change upsets the "norm" that you and those around you had become accustomed to. This isn't always easy. Perhaps you were weak, but now you are strong. Maybe you were shy, but now you are bold. Don't worry, God is with you as promised in Isaiah 43:1-3.

> But now, says the Lord, your Creator, who formed you, "Do not fear, for I have redeemed you; I have called you by name; you are Mine! "When you pass through the waters, I will be with you; And through the rivers, they will not overflow you. When you walk through the fire, you will not be scorched, nor will the flame burn you. "For I am the Lord your God."

CHAPTER TWELVE

Restoration Delays

PROPHETIC INCUBATION

One season that can be missed if not recognized is prophetic incubation. During this season we often see some isolation and separation while God is preparing to raise us into our next assignment from heaven.

When we're about our Father's business, we usually find that a new assignment is exciting and seems to be going well. We have birthed something in the spirit and are enjoying raising up that dream. But then, along comes a quiet restlessness. The challenge just doesn't seem so exciting anymore. Our senses seem dull to the everyday responsibilities of taking care of that which we produced. This is where many people get stuck. They think their purpose is over. They may even think, "I'm done, God can't use me anymore."

However, if we get quiet and pray, we realize that the dreams we birthed have grown up. It's as if they are walking on their own now and don't require much attention anymore. We find that oversight is all that's needed as the particular dream of God is fulfilled. So now what? It's time to birth more dreams! The seeds that God deposited in us are lying dormant, ready and waiting to sprout new life. We start to recognize the new dream and may even give it a name. We get excited about the amazing possibilities for the future. They are limitless because God is limitless! Our spirit becomes awakened once again as a quickening takes place.

At this point, we need to set goals for the future and walk by faith and not by sight. Perpetual vision from the Lord is truly amazing because we know that, "Without a vision the people perish" (Proverbs 29:18). Let's not miss our seasons of life. In the physical realm, it takes nine months for a baby to incubate before it is born. In the spiritual realm, it takes the appointed time. Habakkuk 2:3-4 shows us this, "For the vision is yet for the appointed time; it hastens toward the goal and it will not fail. Though it tarries, wait for it; for it will certainly come, it will not delay. Behold, as for the proud one, his soul is not right within him; but the righteous will live by his faith."

Don't hesitate to ask the Lord to restore dreams that might be lying dormant, just waiting for you to pick them up!

WRONG MOTIVES

If our motives for restoration aren't pure, that could inhibit the process. Since God is a loving God, sometimes He needs to protect us from ourselves. I've known people who wanted to be restored so they could rise to the top, so to speak. They wanted to be great and become well-known, and God knew that their motives were not pure, were not for Kingdom advancement. Fortunately, He never hides our destinies from us, but He may hide them for us. He is our Protector.

Or, let's say we think we're ready for our inheritance to be restored, perhaps millions of dollars. Are we, really? Are we being good stewards with the finances we already have, or have we wasted money on foolish things? What is our motive for wanting to be wealthy?

God knows when we're ready for restoration and multiplication. He makes that very clear in Luke 16:10–12 (TPT):

> The one who manages the little he has been given with faithfulness and integrity will be promoted and trusted with greater responsibilities. But those who cheat with the little they have been given will not be considered trustworthy to receive more. If you have not handled the riches of this world with integrity, why should you be trusted with the eternal treasures of the spiritual world? And if you've not been proven faithful with what belongs to another, why should you be given wealth of your own?

Isn't it wonderful to know that the Lord never, ever gives up on us? He continues to teach, train and restore all the days of our lives. He looks at the heart, and 2 Timothy 4:17 (NKJV) shows us the motive He is looking for: "The Lord stood with me and strengthened me, so that the message might be preached fully through me."

BAPTISM OF LOVE

It was the Father's love that restored mankind to Himself. He sent His only begotten Son to restore, because of love. The spikes did not hold Jesus on the cross – love did. God promises to restore the years the locusts have eaten (Joel 2:25). Some of you have had more locusts devour things in your life than others. Perhaps your marriage or businesses were devoured. It's so important to truly understand that God is love and that He wants to – He longs to – restore. If we do not grasp this, we could inhibit restoration in our lives. Ask the Lord for a baptism of His love and He will give it to you!

FILL YOUR TOOLBOX

Oftentimes, people don't have the right tools to help them succeed. Hopefully, this book will become a part of your spiritual toolbox so that you are filled with faith and ready to believe and receive restoration. There are many more Scriptures on restoration that you can study and make your very own. Fill your toolbox with the Word of God through daily devotions, books, videos and audio teachings about restoration until it becomes a part of who you really are in Christ.

Eat, drink, breathe and contend for restoration for a season, until you see it take place in your life!

- Dream it
- Believe it
- Share it
- Write it
- Plan it
- Do it
- Love it
- Rejoice in it

REFLECTION

Take some time to search your heart and make a list of pure motives for restoration, and present them to the Lord as a gift. Rejoice in God's perfect love for you and thank Him in advance for restoration. There is power in thanksgiving and praise.

Examples:

I want my voice restored so I can sing praises to the King!

I want my finances restored so I can care for the widows and orphans.

CHAPTER THIRTEEN

The Golden Shovel

THE PARABLE

Jesus frequently spoke in parables and still does today. He loves using small stories to illustrate mammoth spiritual lessons. Unfortunately, people often think of parables as simple childhood instructions when in truth they are absolute lifelong applications.

While pondering the *Parable of the Talents* found in Matthew 25:14-30, I saw with my spiritual eyes a huge golden shovel, and the Lord revealed that He wants to dig up buried talents so His sons and daughters can be filled with joy and thrive. When talents are buried, or unemployed, people lose passion and head down a slippery slope of boredom and lukewarmness. Nowhere does the Bible say it is okay to bury talents.

This parable begins with the master leaving for a long journey. He meets with three of his servants and asks them to take care of his possessions while he's gone. He gives the servants, five, two and one talent, respectively. When the master returns to settle accounts with his servants, he finds that the first one did well, immediately investing his five talents and multiplying them to ten. The second servant also acted wisely and now has four talents.

The master is well pleased and says, "'Well done, good and faithful servant. You were faithful with a few things, I will put you in charge of many things; enter into the joy of your master." Unfortunately, the third servant says he was afraid so he buried his talent. The master was furious and said, "To everyone who has [and values his blessings and gifts from God, and has used them wisely], more will be given, and [he will be richly supplied so that] he will have abundance; but from the one who does not have [because he has ignored or disregarded his blessings and gifts from God], even what he does have will be taken away. And throw out the worthless servant into the outer darkness" (Matthew 25:29 AMP).

Of course, in this parable, the servants are us, the church, and the Master is Christ. Talents are everything in our lives that can glorify God – surely our abilities and giftings, but also our resources, time, money, computers, cars, revelation, hospitality, etc. It all belongs to the Lord and He trusts us to care for everything He has given us, as we are honored to be stewards of everything, owners of nothing.

RESTORATION OF TALENTS

God intends for us to administrate His earthly kingdom. It's amazing how much trust God has placed in our hands. Take a look at Psalm 8:3-6 (NKJV):

When I consider Your heavens, the work of Your fingers, the moon and the stars, which You have ordained, what is man that You are mindful of him, and the son of man that You visit him? For You have made him a little lower than the angels, and You have crowned him with glory and honor. *You have made him to have dominion over the works of Your hands; You have put all things under his feet.*

114

Wow! God created the world and put YOU in charge of it. What incredible confidence He has in you. And, isn't it great to know that He will never give you more responsibility than you can handle, as we go back to Matthew 25:15 (NKJV): "To one he gave five talents, to another two, and to another one, to each according *to his own ability*." Even though our Heavenly Master is away for a while, He pays attention to our strengths and weaknesses. He doesn't demand abilities from us that we do not have, but He does demand that we use what He gives us. Using our talents brings Him joy, which consequently brings us joy, because the joy of the Lord is *our* strength.

It's important to realize that in this biblical account each talent was equivalent to a million dollars, so it's a big deal to see the third servant bury his. It's a big deal if we bury ours. The servant here was suffering from fear of failure which can cause self-sabotage. He missed an opportunity to do great things and multiply his talents. Perhaps the servant had developed a bad habit of blame-shifting rather than taking responsibility for his choices. He tells the master that he knew the master was a hard man and he was afraid of him.

In verse 26 of our parable, the master calls the third servant "wicked and lazy." There's good reason for that. It probably didn't take the servant more than five minutes to dig a hole and bury his talent. He saved himself time and energy, but he lost his gift from the Master. Had he just done some research and looked into investment options, he could have learned how to multiply his talent and become the champion he was created to be.

Proverbs 10:4–5 on carelessness should grab our attention:

Lazy men are soon poor; hard workers get rich. A wise youth makes hay while the sun shines, but what a shame to see a lad who sleeps away his hour of opportunity. (TLB)

No one is born with a gold medal around their neck; practice makes perfect (mature). Your talents are precious to your Heavenly Father. If they weren't, He wouldn't have given them to you, and He doesn't expect you to hide them! He expects you to practice using them for the glory of God. After all, your talents are God's gift to you. What you do with them is your gift back to Him.

It's thrilling to know that the church is in a season of restoration. Let's grab that golden shovel and dig up talents that are buried. Don't bow to fear and bury your talents; bury your fear and dig up your talents.

DECLARATIONS

1. I rejoice in restoration and use all my talents to glorify the King of kings.
2. I invest my talents for others; they are not mine to be hidden.
3. I am fruitful, and I multiply.
4. I am a hard worker for the Lord and His purposes, and I will be rich.
5. I steward my talents wisely and they will not be taken from me.
6. I respond to the voice of the Master immediately.
7. I am an ambassador for the Lord and represent Him well.
8. I trust God and serve Him, as He has given me dominion over the works of His hands.
9. I love the Lord God with all my heart, soul and strength and with all my mind. I love my neighbor as myself and serve God with passion.
10. I will stand before my Master and He will say, "Well done, good and faithful servant, enter into the joy of the Lord."

CHAPTER FOURTEEN

Multiplication Time

INCREASE

Restoration includes multiplication. Proverbs 6:31 (NIV) says, "...if he is caught, he must pay sevenfold, though it costs him all the wealth of his house." So, this means increase and upgrades from God!

One day, as I looked around my office, I thought to myself, "I wonder if I have too many projects going on?" I saw a pile of documents for personal taxes, a separate pile for ministry taxes, a pile of messages that needed completion, and Bibles, notes, and other study materials surrounding all of this. The folding sofa was covered with rolls of construction plans for another assignment the Lord has given me, which also requires piles of papers that need to be filled out.

In the next room, a table was covered with photos, T-shirt transfers, and iron-on letters that I need for the shirts I'm making my grandchildren. There were also piles of promotional fliers that needed to be distributed for the ministry, and piles of fliers in the process of being created. There was also a book on Alzheimer's which I needed to study so I could serve a loved one well, and then there were birthday and anniversary cards that needed to get in the mail "yesterday." There were partner lists, prayer lists, reader lists, and grocery lists. My goodness, all the mangers seemed to be full!

The longer I stood and scanned the situation, the more I began to smile. I could only rejoice in the fact that I love being about my Father's business. In fact, the moment I complete a project it seems my spirit is crying out, "Abba Father, what do You want to do next?" Proverbs 14:4 came to mind that day: "Where no oxen are, the manger is clean. But much increase comes by the strength of the ox."

MANGER INVENTORY

How do your mangers look today? Whether it's your school, office, home, or pickup truck, are your mangers full of dirty straw? And how about those calendars? Are they perfectly neat and tidy, or perhaps a bit messy? It seems that things don't always line up as we'd like them to – there are overlapping appointments and choices we must make as to where we're supposed to be at a specific time. Let's face it, life can get cluttered – we can't be everywhere at once. Business here, family there, relationships over here … yet it's all good!

Contrary to the scene I just described to you, I'm not a messy person. I don't like clutter at all, and, as an administrator, I work hard to put things in order. If you were to ask my three adult sons about me, they would tell you that for years I said, "A place for everything and everything in its place." The problem is that I have a lot of things, and a lot of places those things need to be in. I read too many books and study materials to have a clean office. And my ministry unto the Lord, family, and friends are all too important for me to maintain an uncluttered schedule.

That's why Proverbs 14:4 is so encouraging. It says, in effect, that messy mangers are not only okay, but they are very important and necessary to a productive life. If we truly want uncluttered mangers and barns, the solution is easy enough: don't keep any oxen. Unfortunately, however, uncluttered barns are unproductive barns. Well, there we have it – I answered my own question. Do I have too many projects going on? Absolutely not! Rather, I live a restored life. I have a productive and full life, engaging in the work my Father has given me to do. May each task, whether it's lending to the nations or taking a long-stemmed rose to a neighbor, carry eternal value for the King of kings and Lord of lords.

BE CAREFUL WHAT YOU PRAY FOR

There's a real life-key here, contained in the messiness and clutter: if we want expansion, then we must expand. That's what the Word teaches us in Isaiah 54:2, right? We must expand our tent pegs if we want growth! Streeetch … can you feel it? If we are so comfortable that we are not able to expand, then we might be giving the enemy and others a wrong message about our lives. "Okay, I have this neat, little area with a neat, little agenda, and that's the way I intend to keep it." Hmm, that doesn't sound like plans from the God of the universe, does it? Since God is our partner, let's make our plans large – large enough to include Him.

Even though I'm an administrator for the Lord, I take on the extra clutter in all the mangers where my God-ideas are birthed, because, like a farmer, I know it's worth it. More specifically, I know the results will be well worth all the time and attention and clutter that I have put up with. Whether it's a fruitful church, ministry, or life, success doesn't come without a degree of messiness.

Where there are no oxen, the manger is clean. But where God is at work, there is messiness.

Here's a friend's version of Proverbs 14:4 that I laughed at when I heard her say it: "With much increase often comes much crap." As I look at my piles of work that need to be done, files that need to be put away, messages to be completed, and books to be read, I guess I'll just keep smilin' because God is at work in my life – I am restored! And I'm quite positive, if you would look at the messiness of your life, that He is at work in yours, too.

REFLECTION:

Most people are pleasantly surprised when they get quiet and take time to write down all of the good things Christ has multiplied in their lives. Take a look back several years and make a list of things God has multiplied for you. Perhaps peace, patience, kindness, finances, relationships. There are thousands of things to consider. May you be pleasantly surprised at the goodness of our God.

CHAPTER FIFTEEN

From the Valley to the Mountaintops

A CALL TO THE MOUNTAINTOP

As we are restored, it's important not to get stuck in transition. When Holy Spirit whispered to me to teach on this possibility, I had never really thought about people being stuck in transition. Having been a social worker for many years before answering the call of God, I've seen a lot of people get stuck. However, I never thought about, or perhaps didn't realize, some of them were stuck in transition. In other words, the change in their lives was over, but they weren't moving on. That certainly isn't God's will. His will wants the very best for us, and He doesn't want us to live in the valley. He's calling us to the mountain top.

Transition is the process, or portion of time, of changing from one state or condition to another. It is going through a passage, a move, a transformation, a conversion or metamorphosis. While in prayer about all of this, the Lord showed me a mountain range and began to speak about how we transition.

DRY BONES

When we look at Ezekiel's vision found in Ezekiel 37, we do not see the people of God on the mountain. They are in the valley – a valley of dry bones. Now, we can all go through seasons of the valley, but we're expected and empowered to grow in the valley, then ascend and plant the flag of victory on the mountain top. In fact, each time we overcome obstacles and go to the mountain top, it is higher, wider, and more magnificent because God entrusts us to continuously occupy more land until Jesus returns.

I'm telling you, God is about to breathe new life into His people, His army as seen in Ezekiel's vision, and we need to be ready and positioned to receive.

OVERCOMERS

I frequently hear people complain or put themselves down because they sense they are "going around the mountain" again. Oftentimes this is a lie from the father of lies. You're not going around the mountain again. You're growing in the valley. You are an overcomer and will ascend to the hill of the Lord! But if the liar can, he will make you believe you've messed up and, believing the lie, you say something like, "Here I go around the mountain again. For forty years now, around and around, just like the Israelites." Then the liar drags you down and the lie becomes an open door for the DIS–DEMONS to enter in your life:

Dis–Couragement
Dis–Appointment
Dis–Approval
Dis–Connected
Dis–Abled
Dis–Agreeable

Dis–Appear

Dis–Advantage

Dis–Contentment

The truth is, friend, that what's really happening is you're going from mountain to mountain, from glory to glory. However, we don't fly or jump from mountain to mountain – it's a process. Don't resist the process. We should be consistently taking more territory as we occupy all seven spheres of influence or mountains in society (government, education, church, family, marketplace, entertainment, media). The Scriptures are clear saying that we are to be salt and light wherever we go. We occupy the mountains with the love of Christ.

THE RATTLING

Don't miss out. Grow, seek and learn during your restoration. Do you hear the bones rattling, coming together as a powerful army? God's people are becoming aware that a mighty move of God is rattling in the family, government, marketplace and beyond. People are realizing that their vocation is their call, their God-given assignment, and they are lifting their voices, speaking truth. I hear the dry bones rattling as I see millions of students gathering and praying at the pole. I hear the bones rattling when the government takes action to ban abortion on babies over 20 weeks – at least that's a start to preventing millions of more murders. I hear the bones rattling when millions of people gather in Washington D.C. for non-stop prayer lasting four days, and when thousands are praying for God to calm the winds and turn massive storms back to sea!

TRANSFIGURATION

Second Corinthians assures us that we can be changed or transformed from glory to glory, or should we say from mountain to mountain. The Greek word for transformed is *metamorphoō* which means to change into another form, to transform, to transfigure. Wow! Just think; as God restores to you all that's rightfully yours, He wants you to be like Him.

Following the transfiguration, Jesus' appearance was changed and He was radiant with divine brightness. Do you know where this transformation took place? Answer: On the mountain, of course! I'm telling you, as followers of Christ – that's where our transformation will take place, too. That's why restoration unto wholeness is so important. We must be whole and love our neighbors as ourselves, believing that we are the righteousness of Christ and are called to the mountain top.

Here's the transfiguration story for you to ponder in your heart.

Now about eight days after these teachings, He took along Peter and John and James and went ***up on the mountain to pray***. As He was praying, the appearance of His face became different [actually transformed], and His clothing became white and flashing with the brilliance of lightning. And behold, two men were talking with Him; and they were Moses and Elijah, who appeared in glory, and were speaking of His departure [from earthly life], which He was about to bring to fulfillment at Jerusalem.   – Luke 9:28-31 AMP

Isaiah 60 says that we too will arise and shine, literally – shine. That's about as miraculous as restoration can get! Let's stay close to God for and during restoration. God answers prayer and He will meet us on the mountain top. Get ready, stay ready.

OUT OF THE VALLEY

Please allow me to share even more Scripture. It's just so magnificent, and remember, it's active and will restore you!

Look at what Isaiah has to say about your mountain top experiences:

> Climb a high mountain, church. You're the preacher of good news. Raise your voice. Make it good and loud. You're the preacher of good news. Speak loud and clear. Don't be timid! Tell the cities, "Look! Your God!" Look at him! God, the Master, comes in power, ready to go into action. He is going to pay back his enemies and reward those who have loved him.
> – Isaiah 40:9-11 MSG

Do you see it? Restoration equals action. When we are whole, we are the light of the world, radiant with God's glory, following our own personal transfigurations. You are the light of the world, a city on a hill [a mountain] and you cannot be hidden (Matthew 5). And I guarantee that when you come through your own metamorphosis you will want to *shout from the mountain top and give God the glory*. I enjoy how *The Message* paraphrase describes you – and me.

> You're here to be light, bringing out the God-colors in the world. God is not a secret to be kept. We're going public with this, as public as a city on a hill. If I make you light-bearers, you don't think I'm going to hide you under a bucket, do you? I'm putting you on a light stand. Now that I've put you there on a hilltop, on a light stand – shine! Keep open house;

125

be generous with your lives. By opening up to others, you'll prompt people to open up with God, this generous Father in heaven"   – Matthew 5:14-16 MSG

INQUIRE AND GO FOR IT

And David inquired at the Lord, saying, Shall I pursue after this troop? *[troop – raiders, robbers]* Shall I overtake them? And he answered him, Pursue: for you shall surely overtake them, and without fail recover all.   – 1 Samuel 30:8 (KJV)

We've learned a lot about restoration. We looked back for a moment to take inventory of what needs to be restored in our lives. Now, we march forward, because if we look back too long we draw back. Now, it's time to contend! Get your Bible out and declare the Word of the Lord – it cannot return void. Jesus came to give YOU life abundant (John 10:10).

Keep in mind that some things that are restored may not be identical to what the enemy stole. But one thing is for sure, restoration will be good, because God is good.

CHAPTER SIXTEEN

Take Back Your Stuff

OVERTAKE

I love how David asks God a question and, once he receives the answer, nothing can stop him. The enemy had come into his camp and stolen everything he and his men had – not only their possessions but even their families. It was extremely overwhelming. But now, he is full of the power of God and ready to overtake! Just the fact that he inquires of God indicates that he knows God has the answer; God has the victory. If you read the story in 1 Samuel 30, you will find that not only did they recover what was taken, but ended up with much more.

Hopefully, this book has convinced you that God's heart is to restore what you have lost, stolen or given up.

RECOVER ALL

As you move into the recovery state, stay filled with hope and expectation. Expectation is the greenhouse for miracles. Keep believing, keep declaring, and when you've done all – stand. God wants to bless you so you can be a blessing.

SPOIL

The word *spoil* in 1 Samuel 30 means "to plunder or take the goods from the enemy." So, like David, we can not only recover all but can stand on the Word of God for more. Proverbs 6:31 is an amazing word of the Lord regarding restoration:

> Yet when he is found, he must restore [Shalam Strong's H7999] sevenfold; He may have to give up all the substance of his house. – Proverbs 6:31 (NKJV)

REFLECTION

Take some time to journal about how God has shown Himself mighty as the RESTORER in your life. Your testimony is powerful! Not only to you as you document restoration in motion, but also to others as Revelation 12:11 (NKJV) says, "They overcame him by the blood of the Lamb and by the word of their testimony..."

CHAPTER SEVENTEEN

Perception Is Reality

LET MY PEOPLE GO

In Exodus 14 we see God send Moses to Pharaoh, the ruler in Egypt, to tell him he must release God's people from slavery. Pharaoh refused, so God sent ten plagues into the land. Eventually, Moses led millions of men, women and children out of slavery in Egypt and on a journey to their Promised Land. The people would experience many miracles on their journey. The first one recorded is when Moses parted the Red Sea so they could cross safely, while God directed them with pillars of clouds by day and a pillar of fire by night. However, before God's people entered the land of milk and honey, there was scouting to be done.

TIME TO SPY

Let's look at how God operates when He sends us to our promised land, aka destiny.

Then the Lord spoke to Moses saying, "Send out for yourself men so that they may spy out the land of Canaan, *which I am going to give* to the sons of Israel; you shall send a man from each of their fathers' tribes, everyone a leader among them." So Moses sent them from the wilderness of Paran at the command of the Lord, all of them men who were heads of the sons of Israel.   – Numbers 13:1-3

As we read here, Moses sent the men to spy out the land and see if the people who lived there were strong or weak; if there were few or many. He also told the men to bring some fruit of the land back with them. After forty days, the spies returned with clusters of grapes so large they had to use a pole on their shoulders to carry them. They reported that "the land truly flows with milk and honey ... but the people there are giants and we were like grasshoppers in our own sight and in their sight" (v. 27-32).

Following that bad report, Israel refused to enter the Promised Land. They cried and complained, forgetting all the miracles they had just experienced. But Joshua and Caleb, two of the 12 spies, spoke to the children of Israel, reminding them that the Lord delighted in them and He would bring them into their Promised Land (Number 14:6-9).

PERCEPTION IS REALITY

I find it fascinating that we allow our perceptions to become our reality. Whether right or absolutely dead wrong, they are reality ... to us. Here we see ten spies who spotted giants and they released a bad report saying they were like grasshoppers compared to the giants. However, we also see two spies who saw the exact same giants, yet they released a good report, saying, "We can do it! God is fighting for us."

When it comes to restoration, what is your reality, and which category do you fall in? It's crucial to determine this, because Proverbs 23:7 teaches us that, "As a man thinks in his heart, so he is." Remember – ten of the spies believed in their hearts that they were like grasshoppers. Consequently, they never had a chance to slay the giants in their lives. A sad reality, indeed.

THE MIND OF CHRIST – GOD'S PERCEPTION

When we surrender our lives to Jesus, we take that first step out of our own Egypt, out of every type of slavery and every bondage to which we might be enchained. We enter a one-step program from the kingdom of darkness into the Kingdom of Light. That step, and each one following, are meant to lead us into Canaan, our Promised Land, which is our destiny and inheritance.

So, what is that first step of surrender? It's a step of obedience to Jesus. At that moment in time, we begin to line up our thinking with the Lord's thinking. Second Corinthians 10:5 (AMPC) says it like this:

[Inasmuch as we] refute arguments and theories and reasonings and every proud and lofty thing that sets itself up against the [true] knowledge of God; and we lead every thought and purpose away captive into the obedience of Christ.

There you have it. The Lord clearly tells us that if we choose to be obedient to Him, and want to walk in victory over the plans of the devil, we have to learn to take captive every thought, every doubt, all unbelief, every excessive attempt to figure things out, and then line those thoughts up with the Kingdom of God.

We may not see the big picture when we first invite Jesus into our hearts. We just do it because we realize how much He loves us and the price He paid for our freedom. But as we grow, we realize that He wants us to reveal Himself through us. So, all we do needs to be done with Kingdom perspective in mind. Perception is the way things are viewed, the way in which something is regarded, understood, or interpreted.

Perception will always be huge in our lives, because it becomes our reality. In biblical lessons, look at the impact the twelve spies' perceptions had. As we saw above, all twelve saw the exact same thing, yet ten of them returned with bad reports, complaining and seeing themselves as grasshoppers in their Promised Land, while Joshua and Caleb returned to the people with a good report.

What was the outcome? – Because they had led the people into doubt, God determined that their entire generation – themselves included – would die before Israel entered the Promised Land – a 40-year delay! There were only two exceptions … Joshua and Caleb, of course! Forty years later, these senior statesmen led the charge. How do your perceptions impact others?

Second Kings 6:8-23 is another great illustration of perception. It describes how God provides an army of angels leading horses and chariots of fire to protect the prophet Elisha and his servant. But it's only when God opens the servant's eyes that he can see the angelic army surrounding them.

What's your perception of angels helping you? Psalm 34:7 tells us, "The angel of the Lord encamps around those who fear Him."

And what about David and Goliath in 1 Samuel 17? The Philistines were calling for a single combat, and the only person who came forward to slay the Philistine giant was a young shepherd boy. He goes up to Saul and says, "Hey, I'll fight him." But Saul thinks that is ridiculous, telling David he can't fight the giant; he was just a kid, after all. Saul pretty much says, "This is a humongous warrior who could eat you for breakfast!" However, the shepherd boy is adamant, explaining that he's been defending his flock against lions and wolves for years and now he's ready. He's got this! We all know how the story ends.

IT'S A WONDERFUL LIFE

For a more contemporary lesson, let me share a beautiful testimony with you. My precious mother had been in the nursing home for a couple of years, battling Alzheimer's disease and other ailments. One day the hospice nurse called and suggested that if the family wanted to see Mother alive, it was time to gather around her. I immediately caught a flight to Iowa, thinking I'd probably be there a week or so. Well, I ended up being at Mother's bedside twenty-four hours a day for twenty-one days. I learned a deep level of joy and heartache in honoring our parents. When we're young we might honor them because we're told to in the Fifth Commandment, but when we're older we honor them because it's a tremendous privilege.

During my hours with Mother, I asked the Lord for a treasure that I could carry in my heart until she and I meet again in heaven. He sure did answer my prayer. At the end of Mother's time here on earth, she had been without any intake for nine days; no food, no water, nothing. Of course, she was unresponsive at this point, but I knew her spirit was alive and well. I sang "How Great Thou Art" to her and whispered Scriptures in her ear frequently. Three days before mother transitioned to heaven, she opened her eyes. I jumped out of my chair and put my face right in front of hers. I said, "I love you, Mama. Can you see me? Can you hear me?" She spoke as clearly as a bell, "It's a wonderful life."

I almost fainted! I looked at my niece, Jessica Joy, who was also in the room, and I asked if she'd heard mother talk. She had.

Jessica was getting tissues for both of us as we cried tears of gratitude for our treasure.

Now, mother was a woman who worked hard all her life. She was a strong German lady who knew both how to hold her ground and how to love. She lived through World War II and would share stories about the attack on Pearl Harbor.

My mother also shared about how the women took care of the farms and animals when the men went to war. She gathered and washed hundreds of eggs, selling them for income. She raised gardens the size of small fields and fed her family well. I remember having cardboard boxes packed full of dirty laundry when we had no washer and dryer but, somehow, she managed to keep up with a family of seven people.

Mother lived a humble life – she was in a tiny apartment the last years of her life; she rarely ever complained. She enjoyed everything around her and cherished every gift – loving her family, her flowers and her God. From her perspective, it was a wonderful life.

How about our perceptions? Are they positive or negative? Let's ask ourselves how we're doing with our thought-life. We all develop filters that we see through as we journey on this earth. If we don't learn to take our thoughts captive and choose what filters we process through, we can get into big trouble.

WHAT'S YOUR FILTER?

What are some of the filters we process life through? Are they destructive or productive? Are they old wineskins or new?

In Numbers 13 we see the Israelites afraid to confront the enemy. They were sent to scout out the situation, but their filter was fear. "We were in our own sight as grasshoppers, and so we were in their sight" (Numbers 13:33 KJV).

We must learn to process life through the cross, as it's a finished blueprint for us. If we learn to process life through it as a positive filter, we are not conformed to this world, "but are transformed by the renewing of our mind, so that we prove what the will of God is, which is good and acceptable and perfect" (Romans 12:2).

What a marvelous win-win life we can have, because we know that all things work together for good. Take some time and think of current situations in your life, asking yourself, "Am I processing these situations through my perspective or God's perspective? Am I processing them through love? Because God is love."

When we learn to let the Good News be our filter, we become the good news. Philippians 4:8 is a great way to take every thought captive. At any given moment we can ask ourselves, "Is what I'm thinking or doing or saying honorable, right, pure, lovely, sounding well?" If not, then quickly realign.

DO NOT FEED THE GIANTS

What are some of the giants we face as we march toward our own Promised Land – our destiny? Are we brave one moment and fearful the next? If so, we might have a grasshopper complex. The Israelites didn't take doubt and fear captive and they imagined themselves getting squished!

Perhaps your giant is public speaking, the dread of embarrassment, fear of being alone, failure, success, confrontation, change, the unknown? Or how about blind spots, temptations, trials, addictions or weaknesses.

Don't feed the giants! If you tolerate a giant, it will take over your territory.

WE ARE OVERCOMERS

Revelation 2:25-28 encourages us to hold fast, to not give up. It teaches about overcoming. To overcome does not necessarily mean winning the victory over an outside enemy. Many deadly enemies are on the inside. They're called pride, greed, jealousy, anger, deceit, unforgiveness, fear, lust, self-pity, anger, and many others. Our Scripture goes on to say that when we complete the victory on the inside, the Lord will give us the morning star. The morning star here is an explosion of glory following the battles.

You will know when you've overcome your giants – God will give you a deeper love for the nations and a passion for the greatest harvest of souls the earth has ever seen (Revelation 2:26-27).

NO DRAMA ZONE

How do we perceive the issues we go through? Do we turn each situation into a huge crisis or do we see it as an opportunity to grow and be transformed, restored? Each of us has an individual destiny, a divine purpose here on earth, that is our Promised Land. And the church at large has a corporate destiny, also. We find this in Romans 8:29 which says, "For those whom He foreknew, He also predestined to become conformed to the image of His Son, so that He would be the firstborn among many brethren."

Just imagine the power of the army of God arising on the earth to do great exploits. We will not be grasshoppers. We press into God's Word for healing and wholeness, and He sets us free from our giants when our perceptions become accurate, when they line up with the Kingdom of God.

And, we watch all things work together for good (Romans 8:28).

THE PROMISE IS YOURS

It's crucial to take note in Numbers 13:1-2 that God told the Israelite children (and you, since you're grafted in) that the land was already theirs. He was giving it to them, as they trusted Him and were obedient.

Caleb and Joshua were focused on God, they were obedient to God. The Israelites were looking through a negative filter, a filter of fear, and they missed their true identity. They should have looked into the mirror of God and beheld His glory. For, whatever we behold, we become (2 Corinthians 3:18).

When we lose sight of the promises and nature of God, our view [perception] is distorted; it's like losing our eye glasses and things become blurry.

The Israelites had seen God work many miracles since leaving Egypt. They had seen God's power displayed for them at the Red Sea. He supplied food supernaturally daily, and now here they were, camped in the south region of the Promised Land, waiting to enter into the land of milk and honey. They were just reaching their goal and they slipped into doubt and fear. They did not pass the test.

CLAIMING THE PROMISES

Just think, when Caleb was 85 years old it was finally time for him to claim the promise God had made 45 years earlier. And God made sure that age was not a problem. Caleb told Joshua:

> I am as strong this day as on the day that Moses sent me; just as my strength was then, so now is my strength for war, both for going out and for coming in. Now, therefore, give me this mountain...   –Joshua 14:11 (NKJV)

Wow! After almost half a century of waiting, Caleb was still strong; it was time to seize the victory.

POSITIVE PERCEPTIONS LEAD TO POSITIVE RESULTS

God is wanting to increase our faith today. He wants us to enter our Promised Land and bear much fruit. Why do you think God told the spies to bring fruit back for the people to see? Because He wanted everyone to see the richness in the land of milk and honey so it would strengthen their faith and change their perceptions.

The place where the huge bunch of grapes was found was named Eshcol, a word that means "a cluster." The grapes were a clear sign of the fertility of the Promised Land, and a cluster can also be comparable to a collaboration. I believe we are seeing more and more collaboration on the earth as ministries, churches and businesses pull together, locking shields and walking arm in arm to advance the Kingdom of God.

DON'T MISS YOUR TURN

Ten of the spies could not stop talking about the giants living in the land. They talked about how strong the people in the Promised Land were and how it would be impossible to conquer them. The more they talked, the bigger the giants got. They became crippled with fear because of their perceptions.

We can learn from people's crippling mistakes and pray for grace and boldness to step into our own promised land. When we hear negative reports, let's be like Joshua and Caleb and turn them into positive reports, because all things are possible with God (Matthew 19:26). In Numbers 14:24, God said that Caleb had a "different spirit" than the ten spies. While the ten incited the Israelites to fear, Caleb spoke words of truth to the fearful Israelites. He said, "We should go up and take possession of the land, for we can certainly do it" (Numbers 13:30 NIV). Next time – every time – the devil whispers fear and doubt in your ear, remember that he is the father of lies. Go straight to the Bible and find the opposite whisper: Truth – the key to success.

Let's be like Caleb and have a "different spirit." God is referring to a spirit of faith. Faith means not looking at what is visible but believing that God is Almighty and can bring the invisible into the visible. Faith means being obedient even when we don't see the final results. Faith means action. Faith gives results.

Joshua and Caleb paint an exciting prophetic picture for us today, telling us who will be allowed to enter the "Promised Land," and how we can be included in that population.

GIANTS AREN'T MEANT TO DEFEAT YOU; THEY ARE MEANT TO PROMOTE YOU

God wants to promote you much more than you want to be promoted. He longs for His people to enter their Promised Land. Friends, we can't fear false giants; we learn to "walk by faith and not by sight" (2 Corinthians 5:7). So if we're walking by faith, we don't see any giants, we only see grasshoppers as we push every hindrance aside.

I love this quote by Nelson Mandela: "It always seems impossible until it's done." And Eleanor Roosevelt's great idea for conquering giants? She said, "Do one thing every day that scares you."

If you're a believer, the same spirit that raised Christ from the dead lives and dwells in you. God's not a "fraidy cat." God is not sick, He is not poor, and He is not a grasshopper.

If you're not a believer in Christ, today is a great day to become one! Simply invite Him into your heart and admit that you're a sinner. Believe that God sent His only Son to die for you, taking all your sin so you can have eternal life. And confess that Jesus is Lord of your life. You will instantly become a new creation in Christ, washed white as snow and ready to start a whole new life.

Like Joshua, "Let us go up and conquer it." I just love that. Joshua walks in bold confidence in His God. In fact, He acts like it's already done.

Let's go possess the Promised Land that God has prepared just for us. No one else can take it. No one else can have it; it's yours. God already scouted it out and He's saying, "Enter, take possession of what I've already given you."

THE WORD OF THE LORD

As I was writing this message, the Lord gave me a dream.

In the dream, I heard the voice of God, like thunder from heaven, speaking Exodus 23:20,22,29 to me (I'm using the Amplified Bible here for clarity):

> I am going to send an Angel before you to keep and guard you on the way and to bring you to the place I have prepared… I will be an enemy to your enemies… I will not drive them out before you in a single year, so that the land does not become desolate [due to lack of attention] and the [wild] animals of the field do not become too numerous for you. I will drive them out before you little by little, until you have increased and are strong enough to take possession of the land.

Next, the volume changed to a still small voice and I heard God whisper, "There are no giants."

Oh my. There's a good place to say hallelujah right there. Of course, there are no real giants to contend with. In God's eyes, all enemies are grasshoppers. He's God! It's all about perception. With God as our partner, we become the giants – a force to be reckoned with. Jesus has already won the victory and we march on a victorious battleground, possessing the land until He returns.

Full restoration includes full possession of your Promised Land. Now go for it!

REFLECTION

What are some things in your life that appear to be giants but are really grasshoppers when you look through the eyes of God?

CONCLUSION

A Great Day for Miracles

No matter what you are going through, rest assured that we serve a God of restoration. Psalm 8:5 tells us that when God created mankind, he crowned him with glory and honor. *Crowned* here means "to surround like a circle."

Romans 3:23 tells us that because of the fall of man, we all fall short of that glory. However, the glory came down to earth when Christ was born (see Luke 2:9) and was restored. Furthermore, through the crucifixion Christ took on all shame and gave mankind His righteousness; He restored the glory of God to mankind.

This restored glory [all that God has and all that He is] should flow into every area of our lives. God forgives our sins and restores us to eternal life. He sets us free and restores us to the purposes we were created for. He redeems our minds from fear, panic, depression and confusion, and He restores us to power, love, and a sound mind. He gives us everything in abundance; we are blessed to be a blessing. He heals our diseases, restores us to divine health.

Restoration is God's plan for ALL; He doesn't just restore those who fall or those who are sick. His heart is to restore everyone to the purposes He created them for. He prophesies in Habakkuk

2:14 that the earth will be filled with the knowledge of the glory of the Lord, as the waters cover the sea. To put it another way, God's purpose has always been to fill the earth with His glory through mankind, through Christians who are RESTORED and reflect the glory of God.

In John 5:8, Jesus gave the lame man at the pool of Bethesda three commands: to rise, take up his bed, and walk. I know from personal experience that God still commands us today to get up and walk as we cooperate with His restorative processes.

As early as Genesis 3:8 we see the importance of walking, as even God walked in the cool of the day. And spiritually speaking, the Lord is commanding us to rise above earthly ways and to step into heavenly pools of glory, for the glory of God is the divine source of all that's good. Taking up our bed and walking can be figurative or literal, and signifies a way of giving God the glory in our restoration. We are not beggars lying on mats but rather ambassadors of Christ walking and living abundant lives. God wants us to become miracles for the world to see and ask, "How can I know this miracle-working Jesus?"

Bethesda means "the house of mercy" or "house of grace." It is wonderful to know that God's mercy reigns over judgment and that He pours out His grace on withered, dry bones. It is time to stand to our feet and become an exceedingly great army. It is time for us to believe the promises and speak the promises of God. It is time to open our mouths, speaking life to every situation, because we are reminded that "death and life are in the power of the tongue" (Proverbs 18:21). The power of God is released when we release the power of the tongue.

Are you feeling paralyzed by life today, or perhaps blind or lame – physically, mentally, emotionally, or even spiritually? Do you feel like you've been lying by the pool for years, waiting for help, waiting for an angel of God to stir up miraculous healing powers? Well, isn't it fascinating that, after waiting for 38 years, the man who was healed never did get in the pool? Jesus just showed up on the scene, singled him out and made him whole.

Let's ask ourselves that probing question that Jesus asked so many years ago: "Do I want to get well?" Jesus asked the question to identify the need. Is there an addiction, a habit or behavior that you've come to enjoy way too much and don't *really* want to be healed of? We'd better be ready when we answer the question, because healing and wholeness bring tremendous responsibility to walk in the fullness of God and fulfill the Great Commission.

Today is a great day for miracles. Don't just hang out waiting to die. Arise and shine! Fight the good fight of faith. Fight for your life – for YOUR restoration. Get mad at the devil, at the disease, at the poverty – righteous anger. It's a great day to get up and fight the good fight as a champion of God. Jesus is the Restorer; He's the One who will single you out and say, "Hey! It's your turn to rise up and walk." You can recover all and have a wonderful life.

Restoration Declarations

We've discussed many Scriptures about restoration. Now, let's take those Scriptures, the promises of God, and apply them to our lives. Remember, the Word of God is alive, it's active and it must accomplish what it's sent out to do.

> So will My word be which goes forth from My mouth; It will not return to Me empty, without accomplishing what I desire, and without succeeding in the matter for which I sent it. — Isaiah 55:11

As long as we're on this earth we are the mouthpiece of God (First Peter 4:11). May His will be done on earth as it is in heaven. Let's do some sending of the Word. The Lord has spoken to you through His Word, and you agree that restoration is His will and it is needed in your life. Now, take God's Word and write it and speak it as a profession of faith.

In the book of Job, the Bible promises that if we declare a thing, it shall be established. "You will also declare a thing, and it will be established for you; so light will shine on your ways" (Job 22:28 NKJV). "Light" in this verse includes light of day, light of life, light of prosperity, light of instruction. God wants to shine restoration on you.

You can also insert your name into the Scriptures that God illuminates to you.

Here are a few declarations to inspire you:

- Thank You, Lord, for restoring joy to me. Your joy is my strength. You uphold me with your generous Spirit and I will walk in joy, peace and righteousness because that's the Kingdom of God (Psalm 51:12, Romans 14:17).

- I am an heir with the Father and a joint heir in Christ (Galatians 4:6–7; Romans 8:17).

- I co-labor with the Lord as He restores me to wholeness.

- I do not focus on lack, I focus on restoration. Restoration is my filter when life happens.

- God's thoughts toward me are for shalom and not for evil. He plans to give me a future and a hope. He plans for me to prosper (Jeremiah 29:11).

- God will restore to me _____.

- The Lord will restore health to me and heal me of all wounds (Jeremiah 30:17).

- I am a part of the Bride of Christ and am making myself ready for Him as He restores what was stolen by the enemy (Revelation 19:7, John 10:10).

- My God is a restorer of life and nourishes me even in old age (Ruth 4:15).

- My mind is renewed [restored] and I am transformed (Romans 12:2).

- I continuously praise and thank my Heavenly Father who restores my soul (Psalm 23).

- I will rest in my wholeness in Christ.

Printed in Great Britain
by Amazon